VALERY BRIUSOV

AND THE RISE OF RUSSIAN SYMBOLISM

by

MARTIN P. RICE

Ardis   Ann Arbor

Published by Ardis, Inc., 2901 Heatherway, Ann Arbor, Mich.
First printing January 1975. Manufactured in the United
States of America.

TABLE OF CONTENTS

VALERY BRIUSOV AND THE RISE OF

RUSSIAN SYMBOLISM

INTRODUCTION

The Beginnings of Modernism in Russia

On the occasion of its publication in 1894 the
first installment of the anthology *The Russian Symbolists (Russkie simvolisty)* enjoyed a *succès de scan-
dale* entirely out of proportion to its poetic significance. Fifteen years earlier the appearance of such
a book would have attracted little more than a few
words of derision in Mikhailovsky's acrid columns
in *Notes of the Fatherland (Otechestvennye zapiski),*
had it received any notice at all. But in the period
from 1880 to 1894 Russian literary life experienced
a radical upheaval, and when "normalcy" finally returned, literary society found its appearance undeniably and permanently altered.

The reign of Alexander III was a period of
intense reaction during which the revolutionary movement, which had been developing almost uninterrup-
tedly for twenty years, was suppressed with a violence
unmatched since the darkest days of Nicholas I's
suppression of the Decembrists. The first to suffer
under the new regime was the intelligentsia.

It took the revolutionary-democratic critics
from approximately 1847 to 1862 to entrench
themselves firmly as the arbiters of literary taste,
aided, of course, by the relaxed atmosphere of the
reforms under Alexander II. Part of their struggle

[3]

Valery Briusov

for supremacy over the intellectual life of the country involved overcoming the older generation's reaction to their iconoclastic treatment of all that had formerly been sacred in Russian literature. It was only to be expected that the new generation, the generation of the future Symbolists, would in turn react adversely to the intellectual dogma of the sixties and seventies. But the unprecedented swiftness with which the new ideas became predominant must be explained in part by the fact that the "fathers" were fighting for their very existence; they had neither the opportunity nor the means to engage in a polemical duel with the rising anti-civic tendencies being expressed by the new generation.

The reaction was already firmly entrenched in 1884 when, under the all too capable tenure of the Procurator of the Holy Synod, Konstantin Pobedonostsev, two events occurred that marked respectively the end of the old way of life and the beginning of the new in Russian intellectual and literary society. As part of its drive against the revolutionary press, the regime ordered the closing of *Notes of the Fatherland,* the leading organ of the radical intelligentsia, now edited by Nekrasov and Saltykov-Shchedrin. In the same year *The Dawn (Zaria),* a Kiev newspaper, began publishing "alarming" articles by N. M. Minsky (pseudonym of N. M. Vilenkin) and by Ieronim Yasinsky, a minor novelist. These articles, which one critic described as "the first esthetic manifestoes of modernism,"[1] were the initial expression of a new reaction, not political and social, but intellectual and artistic.

These "new ideas" were not new at all; they were really a restatement of the doctrine of "art for art's sake" which had been ruthlessly crushed in the sixties by the civic critics; and they were not only a call for a new emphasis on esthetic pleasure, but also the manifestation of a growing, widespread reaction to Realism, a movement which had

[4]

become intolerably boring and unimaginative, particularly with the advent of many second-rate adherents.[2] The new ideas, as Chizhevsky points out, expressed an "awakening of interest in poetic form, which, in its turn, had been all too often neglected." When Minsky wrote that "to demand from poetry anything besides esthetic pleasure is the same as demanding from the eye not only that it see but hear and smell as well,"[3] the tenacious old men of the seventies, in spite of the heavy government attack underway against them, made an effort to repel this encroaching estheticism. Their defences were weakened nevertheless. By 1891 Shelgunov, Gleb Uspensky, Saltykov-Shchedrin, and Chernyshevsky were dead, and only Mikhailovsky was left to carry the banner of "social consciousness." He was, however, helpless before the developing new tide of modernism. As early as 1883 Afanasy Fet, sensing a change in the literary atmosphere, began to publish again after twenty years of silence. It was as though a flood-gate had opened, and one after another collections by Pleshcheev, Polonsky, Apukhtin, Andreevsky, Ramshev, Fofanov, Frug, Golenishchev-Kutuzov, Minsky, Merezhkovsky, and Yasinsky began to follow in an uninterrupted torrent (Kogan, 73).

According to E. Anichkov, this sudden upsurge of poetic inspiration "grew in Russia out of a dreary emptiness, a spiritual one, out of a stubborn unwillingness to be infected by the dead odor with which the literature of the eighties was impregnated."[4] It was from out of this spiritual emptiness that the "new ideas" were to develop. At this time, however, the one bond which united these men was the overwhelming desire to reintroduce *beautiful* poetry into Russian culture. With the prominent exception of Fet, their poetry was on the whole eclectic and weak in theme and technique, but nevertheless this was the freshly turned soil out of which the Russian Silver Age was to bloom.

Valery Briusov

In order to make its mark on Russian culture the new generation needed a journal which could serve as an outlet for its work and which would be sympathetic to its cause. It found this haven in *The Northern Herald (Severnyi vestnik),* particularly in 1889 when the journal passed to the editorship of A. L. Volynsky (pseudonym of A. L. Flekser). When it was first founded in the mid-eighties by A. M. Evreinova, *The Northern Herald* was hardly thought of as an organ for the new ideas. Mikhailovsky, after the collapse of *Notes of the Fatherland,* joined the staff of *The Northern Herald*, from where he launched his attacks "against those who consciously or unconsciously were . . . allies in 'lowering the spiritual level of society'."[5] It was obvious that he could not long survive surrounded by the very forces he was so desperately trying to annihilate, and soon he moved to the newly-founded *Russian Wealth (Russkoe bogatstvo),* the last gasp of the rapidly fading men of the seventies.

In contrast, it was from the pages of *The Northern Herald* that the first breath of the "new ideas" emanated. Soon the future leaders of Russian Symbolism were all gathered around Volynsky and his journal, and the poems of Merezhkovsky, Z. Gippius, Sologub, and Minsky were appearing regularly in its columns. It was the editorial writing of Volynsky, however, that first gave real evidence that recent rumblings in Russian intellectual and artistic life were based on something greater than a frustrated desire for beauty. Now works such as Minsky's *In the Light of Conscience*—called by Stender-Petersen "the first conscious founding of the emerging Symbolism"[6]— and Merezhkovsky's *On the Causes of the Decline, and on the New Tendencies in, Contemporary Russian Literature,* started to appear. It was at this time, the end of the eighties and beginning of the nineties, that the younger generation began its struggle to articulate its newly discovered worldview. As Merezhkovsky stated it:

The Rise of Russian Symbolism

Our period is characterized by two juxtaposed features—it is
a time of the most extreme *materialism* and also a time of the
most passionate *idealistic* transports of the spirit. We are present at a great, highly significant struggle between two views
of life, two diametrically opposed *Weltanschauungen.* The
latest demands of religious experience are colliding with the
latest conclusions of empirical knowledge. It was impossible
for the intellectual battle with which the nineteenth century
was filled not to be reflected in contemporary literature.[7]

By 1894 these idealistic transports of the spirit
were finding their stunning expression in Balmont's
"praises of the liberating power of dream and love,"
in Merezhkovsky's "God-seeking," and in Sologub's
"sexual ecstasies."[8] Taken as a whole, the work of
these poets, as well as that of others such as Gippius,
Minsky, Vladimir Solovyov, Konstantin Sluchevsky,
and Mirra Lokhvitskaya, constituted nascent Symbolism's expression of its new mystical, religious, and
philosophical sensitivities, the expression of a worldview that rejected and denied the social and civic re-
sponsibilities of the previous generation in favor of
total freedom for the individual and his spiritual
and esthetic yearnings.
This clarion call for self-expression was a reaction against the utilitarian materialism of the older
generation. It remained only for someone to unite
all of these disparate energies into a cohesive whole,
into a movement with the means to consolidate its
early victories and to stabilize its preeminence in
Russian culture. This task fell to Valery Briusov.

CHAPTER ONE

The Early Years (1873-1894)

1. Childhood and Youth (1873-1890)

During the early 1850s Briusov's paternal grandfather, Kuzma Andreevich Briusov, an enterprising peasant from the Kostromskaia Guberniia, purchased freedom for his family and himself and moved from the provinces to Moscow.[1] In the capital the uneducated former peasant managed to establish a business in cork with the help of a small inheritance left him by a brother. At that time there were no other cork firms in Moscow, and the shrewd newcomer rapidly developed a thriving business. Although the undertaking did not always continue to grow at the same brisk pace, by the time of his death the old man was nevertheless able to leave a modest fortune, a profitable concern, and a gloomy old stone house on Tsvetnoi Boulevard.

Life in the old house was anything but joyful, for the narrow provincialism of the Moscow merchant class was everywhere evident. The fare on Kuzma Andreevich's table was meager. He dominated his wife, who dared not raise her voice in his presence but who maintained strict control over the rest of the household. The only reading material in the

house was a dog-eared copy of the *Saints' Calendar,*
and the only company the Briusovs enjoyed was
that of other merchants; their conversation concerned
daily ups and downs in business. It was, of course,
a foregone conclusion that the merchant's son, Yakov
Kuzmich, would eventually take over the business and that
life would continue as it had ever since the family had
moved to Moscow. The times, however, decreed otherwise.

Just as Kuzma Andreevich had become an arche-
typical Moscow merchant, so his son became an arche-
typical "man of the sixties." Like most of the youth
of his generation, Yakov Kuzmich read Pisarev and
other radical writers avidly. As a result of his reading
it did not take him long to realize that his education,
which consisted mostly of "on the job training" in
the family store, was sorely lacking. Consequently,
Yakov Kuzmich, together with some of his friends,
founded a society for self-improvement, and he eventually acquired an adequate, even a broad education.
He became well read in Russian literature, read all
the latest books in the social sciences, studied French,
and took courses at the Petrovskaia Agricultural
Academy. These new-found interests, along with his
growing radicalism, brought a sense of estrangement
from his merchant origins. Among his friends he now
numbered nihilists and revolutionaries. One of the
revolutionary types with whom Yakov Kuzmich was
acquainted in his early "radical" days was Nikolai A.
Morozov, a long-time revolutionary who was responsible in the early 1880s for printing the first Russian
translation of *The Communist Manifesto* in his
journal *The Russian Social-Revolutionary Library*
(Russkaia sotsial'no-revoliutsionnaia biblioteka),
which he published in Geneva.[2]

His parents, of course, thoroughly disapproved
of their son's interests and friends, but they were
more horrified still when he married Matrena Alexandrovna Bakulina, an emancipated young woman with
bobbed hair who had come from the provincial town

Valery Briusov

of Lebedian to the capital in order to become a "new woman." Matrena Alexandrovna had stopped wearing the cross of Orthodoxy around her neck and had begun to frequent the same circles as Yakov Kuzmich. Kuzma Andreevich was never able to forgive his son for marrying that "Godless" woman, but according to most accounts what really hurt him was the fact that she brought no dowry.

Poverty was not the only difference between the Bakulins and the Briusovs. Although Matrena Alexandrovna's father, Alexander Yakovlevich, was a complete failure in agriculture, he remained a man of letters throughout his life. He evidently spent the greater part of his mature life on his estate where he wrote endless volumes of plays, poems, novels, stories and fables. None of these was ever published, but the frustrated writer was always able to find solace in his memories of the day when he had actually seen Pushkin in a St. Petersburg book store. Bakulin was a man of the twenties and thirties, and for him the only true poets were Derzhavin, the "modern" Zhukovsky, Pushkin, and of course Bakulin himself.

Yakov Kuzmich, the "new man," and his emancipated bride were married in 1872. On December 1, 1873 the first of their five children, Valery Yakovlevich Briusov, was born. The intentional selection of this unusual first name marked the beginning of a most unorthodox childhood. Yakov Kuzmich and Matrena Alexandrovna immediately instituted what Briusov's sister has called his "realistic education." Briusov himself later described it as follows: "I was zealously protected from fairy tales and all 'deviltry.' On the other hand, I found out about Darwin's ideas and the principles of materialism before I had learned multiplication. Needless to say, there was no mention of religion in our house: a belief in God seemed to me to be the very same kind of superstition as a belief in brownies and water-nymphs."[3]

Young Valia was taught to read at an early age,

sometime between his third and fifth year, and he
soon made short work of his children's books, most
of which were published by the Russian Froebel
Society and written according to that German edu-
cator's latest theories. From these he advanced to
stories from the natural sciences and then to the
biographies of great men—artists, explorers, and
scientists: before long he began to dream that some
day he too would "without fail become 'great'."[4]
His young mind was receptive, and his imagination
soon led him to act out the adventures he had read:

> In my games I began to picture myself as a traveler in un-
> known countries and as a great inventor. I liked to construct
> a flying projectile. I would build it out of books and pieces
> of wood and would fly about the rooms with it. Tables and
> chests were mountains, and the floor was the sea where I
> was often wrecked and where I would come upon an unin-
> habited island—the rug. I would live like Robinson Crusoe
> .... From the same time I began to dream about my future
> as about the future of a great man, and I began to be enticed
> by all the vagueness in the versatile word "Glory."[5]

This make-believe world also compensated him
for the absence of any playmates. Because of circumstances—the next child in the family was not born until he was four—and later because he had already become accustomed to being alone, Briusov developed
into a shy and lonely child. This shyness, which made
it very difficult for him to make friends, was a personality trait responsible for much unhappiness in the
future. To occupy himself he read more and more
passionately and was soon devouring books as most
children devour sweets. Since his father believed that
"special children's literature" should not exist and
that there should be no difference between the reading of children and adults, the boy was free to read
anything he desired from his father's many books
and from the multitude of journals to which the
family subscribed. Before long, in addition to his

beloved stories of the "Martyrs of Science," young Briusov began to read any novel he could get his hands on:

From the biographies of great people it was not a difficult transition to the novels of Jules Verne, and then to Cooper, Mayne-Reid, Marryat, and Aimard. Their books, too, produced the strongest of impressions of me. But along with them I was reading French boulevard novels . . . and at the same time all the scientific books that came to hand: Mitchell's *Heavenly Bodies,* Darwin's *Origin of the Species,* Medvediev's *Mineralogy,* and even Niemeyer's *Individual Pathology and Therapy.* Finally, at that same time, when I was about eight years old, I read Dobroliubov and Pisarev for the first time.[6]

It is not surprising that no poets were included in the list of Briusov's favorite authors, for in the "realistic" Briusov household there was little interest in poetry. The lone exception was Nekrasov, of whom Valery's parents stood in awe; and Nekrasov was apparently the first poet whose works he read. He even learned a great many of his poems by heart. The only other poetic works which Briusov read were a few isolated pieces by Lermontov, Polonsky, and Pushkin which he found in various children's anthologies.

Despite appearances, the "realistic" education practiced by Briusov's parents seems to have consisted in allowing the lad to do anything he desired:

Mother and Father evidently considered that the children's lives should proceed according to their own plan. The ideas of the 'sixties,' 'nihilism,' and familiarity with the revolutionary populists left some trace of free thinking, mixed, it is true, with the vestiges of the old traditions of our parents' lives. There was, of course, no conscious idea of 'liberal education': the adults simply lived their lives and the children theirs—[the children] themselves thought up their own games, themselves looked after their studies.[7]

As a consequence of these unsupervised formative

years, Briusov rapidly developed into an "extraordinary, lively, ingenious, and unusually intelligent child,
but, as the first born [he] was unbelievably spoiled.
'Among his positive qualities in childhood it was impossible to include modesty and obedience'."[8] This
lack of modesty and obedience in the child was to
become later a pronounced characteristic in the man.

Although Briusov's chief occupations during the
first ten years of his life were reading, play acting,
and conducting "scientific experiments," he also
wrote his first poetry at the age of eight in 1881.[9]
The versatile youngster by no means limited his literary activity to poetry, however, and in 1881 he
also began to write *A Novel of Sea Life* and "to publish" a journal, *Distant Lands.*[10] Briusov published
his first lines, a letter to the editor of a children's
magazine, *Sincere Word (Zadushevnoye slovo),* in
1884 at the age of ten. The letter was a description
of the village of Medvedkovo near Moscow where the
Briusovs had spent the summer at a cottage. This
same summer also marked Briusov's first close contact with other children, an experience which proved
to be so painful that the future poet contemplated
suicide:

This first attachment [to friends] ended for me in the same
way as many others: disdain from those whom I liked. Having read my fill of stories about the invincible nomads of the
deserts, I also considered myself invincible. My born softness
and pliancy, however, somehow kept me for a long time from
any serious fight with my comrades. But this inevitably had
to happen when I became acquainted with [the local boys],
among whom fist fights were in high esteem. A certain K., an
older boy, persistently challenged me to fight and I did not
refuse. But I was completely inexperienced in such affairs.
K. punched me in the face, knocked me down, and sat on me.
I remember the feeling to this day . . . . Then he asked: "Do
you admit you're defeated?" I said: "I admit it." He let me
go and I left. I ran to the park, climbed a tree, and sat there
in horror, trying to explain to myself what had happened. It
seemed to me that everything had perished, that I no longer

Valery Briusov

> dared to look at people. I wanted to go to the Yauza and drown myself. I even composed a suicide note. (I had often contemplated suicide even earlier.)[11]

This event was an isolated experience in the boy's sheltered life, but eventually the time arrived when young Briusov had to leave the secure haven provided by his home and attend the Gymnasium. The "realistically" raised boy's second contact with the real world was so disturbing that it was years before Briusov was finally able to adapt himself to his surroundings.

Briusov's formal education began with the hiring of a governess, Nastasia Nikolaevna, when he was six years old. She was the first in a long line of almost indistinguishable governesses, all of whom contributed little to his knowledge. They served rather as occasional companions for the lonely boy while he continued to raid his father's library. It did not take long for young Briusov to realize that he was better read than most of his governesses: this fact, combined with his dreams of future greatness, raised considerably his self-esteem: "As before I continued to consider myself quite knowing and clever. Incidentally, this was reinforced by one of our governesses, a certain Liubov Alekseevna, not a very clever woman. I myself overheard her telling someone: 'When Valia [Briusov] tells me something I know that it's so.' It is not surprising that such words did not diminish my self-opinion."[12]

The absolute freedom of choice in his reading did little to prepare Valia to take the entrance examination for Frants Ivanovich Kreiman's Gymnasium in the fall of 1884. Briusov maintains that he was admitted to the second class only because "F.I. Kreiman was ready to accept anyone" (p. 26). He would have been better off if he had placed in the first class, for by now the boys in the second form had been together for a year, and a newcomer was considered more of an intruder than anything else.

[14]

Briusov's troubles were compounded by his igno-
rance of his classmates' language and of the games
they played. He knew neither how to swear nor how
to take part in their play during recesses. Even worse,
he was still unable to defend himself. Once the
others realized this, Briusov's life consisted of one
beating after another, sometimes as often as "six
times a day" (p. 29). Briusov's studies were no more
successful than his relations with his schoolmates.
Before long he was at odds with his instructors in
religion, Latin and German, and evidently the head-
master himself felt no particular love for Briusov
because of the negative reports that came flooding
into his office from the boy's disgruntled teachers.

The one bright spot academically in Briusov's
first year at Kreiman's Gymnasium was the geography class of Egor Frantsevich Vipper. In his pre-
school years Briusov had often invented fictitious
countries, their peoples, and their histories and had
written compositions about them in the form of
"Histories." These "Histories" were illustrated with
maps of continents and drawings of city plans as
well as sketches of costumes and architecture. By
the time he entered school, Briusov had done much
drawing, and although he never had formal lessons,
he was evidently a more than adequate artist.[13]
It is therefore not surprising that his instructor in
penmanship and drawing, I. A. Aleksandrov, admired
the new pupil. He respected Briusov's "accuracy
and patience" as well as his talent. With his teacher's
encouragement, the future poet dreamed for a time
of becoming an artist.

Meanwhile Briusov's loneliness continued. His
first friend at school, a boy named Kormilitsin, soon
abandoned him to join the other, more "lively"
boys. His next two friends were a Jew and the school
clown, both misfits like himself. Briusov's relationship with the Jewish boy, Yulius Arnshtam, was a
particularly emotional one:

Valery Briusov

There at the Gymnasium I experienced the feeling of love. The object of my passion was a boy . . . pretty as a girl, in short pants and with a ribbon instead of a tie. .....He too was rejected. Because of a sickness, not very rare among children, he had irretention of uring and this led once to a very unpleasant event in class. They laughed at him and hit him. My soul, seized with great empathy for all the injured, fell in love with him. I silently followed him, a thousand times I was ready to throw myself on his humiliators and to defend him, but I never did. Suddenly Yulius was absent. He stopped coming to the Gymnasium. . . . Days passed, he did not come. I was seized with a mad desire to see him, to tell him that I loved him. But he did not come. In the evening I would cry at home in bed at the thought that I should never see him. Mornings, in the Gymnasium hall, at common prayer, I would get on my knees and in my unbelieving prayer would say: "God, let Yulius come!" And he came just as he had been, in the same short pants and long lilac stockings, with a ribbon around his neck and with his haughtily raised upper lip. On that very day I started to talk to him, I conquered my habitual shyness. For three days I lived in bliss. We three—I, Stroev [the clown] , and Yulius—the three rejected ones, would wander together in the hall. But this love, too, paid me back with scorn. Yulius began to take up with our comrades, he began to avoid me, and later the day came when I overheard vile mockery from his lips. Yulius! You are now probably a grown man, you are probably occupied with business, are married, have children. If you happen to read this, then know, you were my first love. Yulius! Yulius! (pp. 29-30).

Finally, however, Briusov was able to make friends with several of his fellow students, but only on the basis of his youthful erudition. Briusov had begun relating to Kormilitsin the plots of some of the novels he had read. Eventually other students began to gather about during these story-telling

periods at recess. Before long Briusov found himself
actually preparing at home for these sessions (at the
expense of his school work, of course) and reveling
in being the focal point of such gratifying attention.
After a time his fame spread so far that even students
from the other classes would come to hear him tell
the stories of Jules Verne, Dumas, Mayne-Reid, and
others. Thus the end of Valia's first year at Kreiman's
Gymnasium drew to a close. The following years
were not to be as difficult for him as the first, but
he never grew to feel completely at ease at Kreiman's
and as before he continued to occupy himself more
with his own interests than with the activities pre-
scribed by his instructors and the curriculum.

The major event in Briusov's second year at
school (in the third class) was his sudden interest in
history. Now that he was occupied with history at
a more sophisticated level, he again began to devise
histories of imaginary peoples: "Later my passion
for systematization led me to compile charts for my
imagined history, chronological, statistical, and so
on. I composed histories of the literatures of the
various countries and anthologies of the most remarkable literary models of these lands" (p. 36).
Briusov's intense interest in ancient history explains
his sudden success in Latin, which had formerly
been one of his poorest subjects. He was particularly fascinated by the writings of Caesar, which he read
in Latin and then in Russian translations, and soon
the would-be historian was writing imitations of
Caesar's histories. By the time he reached the fourth
class Briusov had written a story from the times of
the Gallic Wars entitled *Two Centurians*, "and a
large article about Caesar under the title of 'The
Abductors of Power' " (p. 38). It seems likely
that these interests were the source of his eventual
inspiration in writing his two novels in later life,
The Altar of Victory (Altar' pobedy) and *The Fiery
Angel (Ognennyi angel)*, both of which were thought

Valery Briusov

by some critics to be actual historical documents.

In his second year at school Briusov became friendly with Vladimir Staniukovich, one of his fellow classmates. This was to become his first enduring friendship. The relationship, however, had a more significant result: together with Staniukovich Briusov began to publish a handwritten journal called *The Beginning (Nachalo)*, and his participation in this venture led him to conclude at the age of thirteen that he was "above all a man of letters" (p. 34). Even though he had already been actively engaged in writing poetry, it was not until his friendship with Staniukovich that Briusov learned the mysteries of versification. When Briusov suddenly decided that writing was his true vocation, his school work began to suffer more than ever. His literary output at this time knew no generic or thematic bounds; he wrote poems, stories, and articles on subjects ranging from Indian adventures to love stories and stories from the times of the early Romans. When the other students, who made up the young journalists' audience, began to lose interest in the writing published in *The Beginning*, Staniukovich abandoned the enterprise, but Briusov continued to publish the periodical, of which he was now the sole author and probably the only reader. Briusov's love for literature not only did not wane, it became ever stronger:

My passion for literature continued to grow. I would ceaselessly begin new works. I wrote poems, so many that soon I had filled an entire notebook [entitled] *Poésie* which had been given to me as a present. I retried all forms—sonnets, terzas, octaves, triolets, the rondeau, and all meters. I wrote dramas, stories, and novels. I was more carried away every day. On the way to the Gymnasium I would think up new works: in the evening, instead of studying my lessons I would write. I did no translations but painstakingly would recopy my finished works. I eventually collected a huge packet of written sheets (p. 35).

As a result of this feverish literary activity, Briusov
was forced to spend a second year in the fourth
class.

Finally, in 1889, at the age of sixteen, he published his first original article (if we discount his
letter in *Sincere Word* at the age of ten). Oddly
enough, this first article concerned neither literature, history, nor geography. It was a short piece on
horse racing and appeared in *Russian Sport.* Briusov's
father, who had given up his revolutionary ways
when it became apparent that they resulted in finan-
cial hardship, had returned to his father's business and
had become a racing fan; he eventually used the
greater part of his income to maintain a large stable
of horses. Young Valia now an avid follower of the
track also, soon knew all the horses and their
records as well as the records of the jockeys. His
article dealt with parimutuel betting, which was new
at the time in Russia and the main topic of conversation among all racing buffs.[14] In 1891 Briusov
published a second article on sports, this time with
a mathematical slant, in *The Sports Sheet.*

Writing was not young Briusov's only passion,
however. His first experiences with girls date from
his stay at Kreiman's. He tells us that he first experienced sexual arousal when he was six or seven years
old; at that time he would play games with his two
younger sisters, Masha and Klavdiia, in which he too
would take the part of a little girl: "we would ex-
pose ourselves to every sort of [imagined] danger
and torture but bravely survived them all" (p. 21).
By the time he was in school, his "idée fixe" was
to have a relationship with a woman, any woman,
as long as he could seduce her. The first object of
his seductive urge was one of his governesses, a
certain Zoia; the result of all his anguished maneuvering was a stolen kiss on the neck. When he finally did find himself in a room with a woman his
courage sufficed only to drink a bottle of wine with

Valery Briusov

her, pay her two rubles, and leave. Later that same
year he again took a prostitute to a hotel room, and
this time the purpose of the meeting was achieved.
Unfortunately, the results were hardly what young
Valia had dreamed of so long and so ardently: "I tried
to convince myself that this was that moment for
which I had so long waited, but it was all agonizing,
empty, and stupid. Taking my leave I was filled with
sadness. I was disappointed to the depths of my soul"
(p. 42). This first adolescent sexual experience with
a woman was the beginning of Briusov's first period
of prolonged dissipation. By the time he was thirteen
he no longer received any parental supervision at
home. The family situation was grave: Briusov's
father had incurred great debts and was drinking
heavily, and Briusov's little brother, Nikolai, was
seriously ill—he was to die at the age of ten. As a consequence no one paid the slightest attention to the
comings and goings of the wraith-like gymnasium
student. He began spending most of his nights in
brothels and cafes with a group of like-minded comrades from the Gymnasium. He was paying less attention than ever to his studies, and even his interest
in writing flagged.

By the age of fifteen Briusov's position among
his classmates had changed. Now he was an upper-
classman, and there were many younger boys in school
who, because of their age and class, dared not treat
him with scorn. By this time, through a conscious effort to change his personality, he had also acquired
the reputation of an eccentric, a boy who wrote
poetry but who was constantly in trouble with the
school authorities. The shy, retiring boy had become
by his own admission an "impudent snob" (p. 64).
He began to engage in raucous public displays of daring, and with his companions accosted strange ladies
in the street, using the cover of darkness to insult
them both verbally and physically. From all accounts
the reticent poet turned into a rude, obnoxious bully

who was even expelled from social functions for his
impudence. His courage was bolstered by the heavy
drinking in which he now engaged. During the next
three years he frequently became intoxicated and
often ended his nocturnal wanderings by falling into
his bed in a drunken stupor.

At school the other boys recognized that in
spite of his poor grades and reputation he knew considerably more about a greater variety of subjects
than the brightest of them. Moreover, he always had
plenty of money in his pockets, and he spent it freely.
Finally, he was an articulate supporter of republican-
ism and atheism, and he did not hestitate to expound
his views to his fellow students. It was Briusov's political activity which ultimately led Kreiman to ask his
father to withdraw the lad from school. Briusov was
in no way saddened by his imminent departure from
a school where his reputation among his teachers—
both scholastically and politically—was in disrepute
and where he had taken up with the worst element
among the students. He welcomed the opportunity
to "start off fresh" in a new school where he was unknown. In preparation for his new beginning he set
about diligently in 1889 to prepare for the entrance
examinations for L. I. Polivanov's private gymnasium. Although just before his departure from Kreiman's he had practically ceased writing altogether,
he nevertheless continued to read as voraciously as
before. His reading now included Buckle, Curtius'
history of Greece, Georg Gottfried Gervinus on
Shakespeare, and Lessing's *Hamburgische Dramatur-
gie.* As before, he continued to read "from cover to
cover" all the journals regularly subscribed to by his
father.

2. Polivanov's Gymnamsium. Early Literary Activities and the Discovery of Symbolism (1890-1894)

In the fall of 1890 Briusov passed the entrance

examination for Polivanov's school and began attend-
ing lectures in the sixth class. This change in schools
radically affected Briusov's life, but it is doubtful
that any single incident was responsible for the profound change in the young poet's personality at this
time; rather a variety of circumstances seems to have
conspired in this transformation. He spent the summer before his entrance examination in total freedom—
he was not subject to parental supervision, as noted
earlier, nor did he have to attend classes. Thus he was
able to indulge fully in the various forms of debau-
chery which had become a way of life—to such an
extent that he gradually became inured to the "for-
bidden pleasures" that had once held such fascination
for him. Moreover, he was growing older and beginning
to mature socially as well as to develop his intellectual
precocity. In his new surroundings it was no longer
necessary for him to live up to the reputation he had
unfortunately made for himself at Kreiman's, the reputation of a trouble-maker, a poor student, a snob, and
a dissipated dandy. Furthermore, the intellectual cli-
mate of Polivanov's was entirely different from that
of the first school he attended. Polivanov's was a gymnasium which stimulated intellectual curiosity and
rewarded originality and creativity—in a word, a
school much more suitable for a creative youth like
Briusov than had been Kreiman's where, with very
few exceptions, only drudgery and rote learning
were expected, indeed desired.[15]

Although he still made no close friends, Briusov
was able to make the acquaintance of many young
men who were seriously interested in culture, politics
and literature.[16] Briusov's writing evoked from them
not laughter but sincere interest and respect. In this
atmosphere Briusov soon improved in his studies
and became known as "one of the school's best
students." In addition to his former interests he was
now fascinated by mathematics, and he even
selected it for his future major at the university,

but a relatively poor showing in his final examinations—probably as a result of over-confidence—made
the budding mathematician change his mind before
entering the university. Briusov nevertheless maintained his love for mathematics for the rest of his
life, and in his later years he often solved equations
for relaxation. This predilection for the cold logic of
numbers is not surprising in the man whom Bely was
later to call the poet "of bronze and marble" and
whose love for systematization had led him to collect
all the variants of his poetry at the age of eighteen.

Briusov's love for mathematics, like most of his
passions and eccentricities, has been greatly overem-
phasized. Those who scorn him as a poet point to this
lasting avocation as proof of inspirational poverty,
reasoning that a mathematician is a cold, rational
logician whereas a poet, a true poet, is flammable,
impulsive, and illogical. On the other hand, in
Briusov's love of precision one can discern an affinity with Pushkin and his classical predecessors; parallels can also be drawn with Bely—not the dancing,
singing, eccentric young poet of the public appearances, but with the painstaking, almost drudgingly
perservering scholar who labored endlessly over his
systematizations, tables of symbols, and his theories
of versification. It is undoubtedly this predisposition
to system and logic that inspired Briusov in his many
future efforts in the field of poetic theory and in
his continual experimentation with unusual forms
of versification. It is not remarkable, therefore, that
while at Polivanov's, along with his growing interest
in mathematics, Briusov embarked on his first serious
study of philosophy. He heard lectures in the history
of philosophy while at the Gymnasium and was particularly impressed by Kant, Schopenhauer, and, above
all, Spinoza. He went so far as to write "an extensive
commentary" on Spinoza's *Ethics,* and he made a
"key" to the *Ethics* so that he could instantly find
what Spinoza had to say on the subjects of "love

[23]

Valery Briusov

and glory," among others.[17] Briusov's departure
from Kreiman's also marked the end of his first decade of poetic endeavor. His wife has written that if
one were to print all of the poet's manuscripts, beginning with his first poem to approximately 1890,
they would fill "entire volumes."[18] In 1891 the
eighteen-year-old poet collected all of his works,
starting with his initial creation, "The Nightingale,"
written in 1881. He entitled the first notebook of
the collection: "My poems. A collection of all my
poems and drafts from 1881. Valery Briusov.
1891." Inside the cover the notation continues:
"Here are collected all my surviving poems, even be
they insignificant, incomplete excerpts, or the first
poetical babbling of an eight-year-old child (I was
born in 1873). Hereunto is also attached a list of all
my surviving prose works. For my work plans and
plots see my notebook of 1890. Valery Briusov."[19]

This painstaking bibliographical care is further
evidence that young Briusov was convinced that he
would eventually become famous. Usually he accompanied his works with bibliographies, and he appended
variants and dates for the poems included in a given
collection, much as though he were publishing an academic edition. In the "Introduction" to his *Complete
Works* published in 1913 he writes:

To several volumes [of my *Complete Works*] —this refers particularly to the collections of poems—I have appended not
only "bibliographic notes" (which, of course, were easier for
me to compile than for anyone else), but also a small collection
of "variants" [that is] of poems which had undergone changes
during the reissue of separate editions. I request the reader
not to see in this an excess of authorial self-esteem, which
attempts to lend value to every line written by him; but now
that the time has come for me to consider my past [work]
critically, and when I reread after a long interval of time different versions of one and the same poem, I do not always
find the last one to be the best. . . . But, for the benefit of
bibliographers, if they should ever please to look favorably
upon my works, I might add that for them there still remains

a broad field of activity. The bibliographical notes and variants provided by me comprise only an insignificant dole of
that which—if they should desire—can be discovered in the
first editions of my books and in old journals. I do not at all
want to deprive the bibliographers of the pleasure of discover-
ing new poems by Valery Briusov because for the true biblio-
grapher it is, of course, all the same whether the poems he
"discovers" are good or bad: it is only important that they
had previously been unknown. For this last joke I trust that
my readers will excuse me, remembering the words of
Schopenhauer, that "whatever the page may be, it must
not be too serious for a joke in our entirely equivocal life.[20]

This mixture of serious scholarship, arrogance, and
mockery—Briusov's trademark once he had attained
fame—originated with the absolute seriousness with
which he had approached his own work as an adolescent, and the "impudent" posture he had culti-
vated in the gymnasium.

In 1887 Briusov's poetic output began to give
evidence of his future prolificacy. Once more reaf-
firming his chosen path in life, he used the following
lines from Pushkin as an epigraph to the poems of
1887: "Excuse me cold sciences,/ Excuse me games
of my first years!/ I have changed, I am a poet...."[21]
The contents of Briusov's notebooks from these years
have not yet been published; they are, however, described in Gudzii's article "Valery Briusov's Juvenilia"
("Iunosheskoe tvorchestvo Valeriia Briusova"). These
descriptions prove quite relevant and revealing for
the poet's future development. In the favorite themes
of the fourteen-year-old Briusov we frequently find
a reflection of his favorite school subjects, for example, poems related to geography, such as "Vesu-
vius," "Australia," "Italy," and so on. In 1887 he
wrote a poem entitled "Song of the Trojans" a reflection of his growing interest in ancient mythology.
Also among his preferred themes of this period are
the typical tragic-romantic motifs of adolescence—
disenchantment with the world, rejection by others,

Valery Briusov

and unrequited love.[22] During this period he also
began to experiment with poetic form, a subject
about which he was later to write several scholarly
works. In 1889 he wrote his first octave, sonnet,
and triolet.

In his youth Briusov's two favorite poets were
Nadson and Lermontov, and he would frequently
combine Nadson's form and rhymes with Lermontov's themes. On occasion we can see evidence of
attempts to imitate the work of Pushkin, A. K.
Tolstoy, and Fofanov. It was not until much later,
however, that Briusov studied Pushkin seriously,
eventually "completing" the latter's "Egyptian
Nights." Finally, in 1890, Gudzii notes that a strong
autobiographical strain, particularly with reference
to his real or imagined love affairs, becomes predominant in his work (p. 205).

The epithet most often applied to Briusov is
"the industrious poet" (*poet trudoliubiia*) or, as
ironically expressed by Marina Tsvetaeva, "the hero
of labor." Ironically applied or not, it is quite apt
when we note that merely from June, 1890 to April,
1891 Briusov wrote some *two thousand* poems as
well as dozens of short stories, articles, essays,
sketches of novels, and translations.[23] Unlike
Chekhov, who began by writing hundreds of stories
each year but ended his career by only writing four
or five annually, Briusov's early pattern of diligence,
which bordered on compulsive mania, continued
throughout the rest of his productive life.

It was also while at Polivanov's that Briusov's
literary interests widened. He now embarked on
his first real study of Russian literature and in one
year read "all of Turgenev, L. Tolstoy, Dostoevsky,
Pisemsky, Leskov, Ostrovsky, and Goncharov."[24]
At the same time, he deserted his previous poetic
idols, Nadson, Lermontov, and A. K. Tolstoy, substi-
tuting for them his contemporaries , Fofanov,
Merezhkovsky, and the most strident voices of the
"new poetry." in France.

The Early Years

The future leader of the Russian Symbolists had discovered his French predecessors in Symbolism at approximately the same time that he began studying at Polivanov's. Their effect upon him was immediate and profound:

Around the same time (that is, around 1890) I first became acquainted with the poetry of the French Symbolists: with Verlaine, Mallarmé, and Rimbaud. This was a complete revelation for me: not being familiar with Western-European literature of the last half-century, I was able to understand from their lyrics only how far poetry had departed from the Romantics. Everything that had been attained by the Parnassians and Realists of the sixties, everything that had been done by the Pre-Raphaelites and Tennyson's school, of course in vague echoes, reached by ears from Verlaine's early poems, from the considered lines of Mallarmé, and from Rimbaud's youthful pranks. The influence of Pushkin and of the "old" Symbolists capriciously merged within me, and I would seek the classical severity of the Pushkinian verse and dream of that new freedom which the French poets had obtained for poetry. In my verses from that period (also not published) these influences crossed in the most unexpected manner.[25]

Other evidence indicates, however, that Briusov is probably stretching the point when he asserts that he was initiated into Symbolism "around 1890." In *From My Life (Iz moei zhizni)* he writes: "Meanwhile word of the French Symbolists reached literary circles. I read about Verlaine in Merezhkovsky (*On the Causes of the Decline* . . .), then elsewhere in small articles. Finally Nordau's *Entartung* appeared and in Russia Z. Vengerova's article in *The Messenger of Europe (Vestnik Evropy).* I went to a bookstore and bought Verlaine, Mallarmé, A. Rimbaud, and several linck's dramas" (p. 76). Merezhkovsky's article was published in 1893 (Briusov had already read the former's book of poems, *Symbols*, in 1892). Vengerova's article, "The Symbolist Poets in France: Verlaine, Mallarmé, Rimbaud, Laforgue, Moréas" appeared in

Valery Briusov

1892; Nordau's *Degeneration (Entartung)*
was available in Russian in 1893. Thus we can date
Briusov's first real knowledge of Symbolism, not at
"around 1890," as he claimed, but at around 1892
to 1893.[26]

Z. Vengerova's article—a concise survey that
described and characterized the chief traits of
France's leading Symbolists, Verlaine, Mallarmé,
Rimbaud, Laforgue, and Moréas—must have greatly
stimulated Briusov's imagination. Her concluding
remark, " . . . Symbolism, which has given [us the
works of] Verlaine, Mallarmé, and Moréas, must
be recognized as one of the most fruitful schools in
new French poetry,"[27] was taken as gospel by
Briusov. Certainly the success of *Symbols* and the
praise by its author, Merezhkovsky, for Fofanov
provided support in Briusov's eyes for Vengerova's
contentions. That Briusov's commitment to Symbolism as a school of poetry was complete by 1893
is clear from his diary for that year: "February 18:
I didn't go to the Gymnasium. I was preparing a
report on Symbolism. March 1: I am translating
Mallarmé and getting ready to take the translation to
the editor."[28] On March 4 he entered his famous
prophecy concerning his own future and that of
Russian poetry:

Talent—even genius—will, honestly [applied] , yield but slow
success, if it yields it at all. That is not enough! That is not
enough for me! I must choose something . . . I must find a
guiding star in the fog. And I see it: It is Decadence. Yes!
Whatever else one may say—it is false, or it is funny—it is
going forward, it is developing, and the future will belong
to it, particularly when it finds a worthy leader. And that
leader shall be I! Yes, I! (p. 12).

The entries continue in the same vein:

March 10
Today . . . I personally took my translation of Mallarmé

[28]

to the editors of *The Russian Review (Russkoe obozrenie)*.

March 22
What if I were to take it into my head to write a treatise on
spectrum analysis in the language of Homer? I would not
have sufficient words or expressions. It's the same thing if
I take it into my head to express the sensations of the *fin
de siècle* in the language of Pushkin! No, Symbolism is what
is needed!

March 26
I bought *Poètes maudits* [articles by Verlaine on the Symbo-
lists]. Upon recollection I see that I had a great influence in
the Gymnasium. In the spring I was carried away by Spinoza
The *Ethics* appeared everywhere and Yakovlev himself became a Pantheist. In the fall I tackled Merezhkovsky. Everyone began to read *Symbols*. Now I am a Decadent. And Io,
Satin, Kamensky, Yasiuninsky and many others are praising
Symbolism. Bravo![29]

Thus, by March, 1893, Briusov not only saw himself
as the future leader of Symbolism in Russia, but
indeed as the man who had already gathered together
the reins. His literary activities of this time were
already showing his hallmark of studied disregard for
the public morality so characteristic of his early
"decadent" period (as he calls it in his diary). In
1893, for example, he completed a play called *Summer Passions (Dachnye strasti)* and submitted it to
the censor. The play was not passed and in the commentary on his decision the censor wrote:

While depicting dirtyish amourous adventures at a summer
cottage, the author, apparently not familiar with the con-
ventions and proprieties of the stage, has lent his play an
excessively obscene, and in places cynical character. The
young people introduced by him, who kiss and embrace girls
on garden benches, declare quite openly that they have not
the slightest intention of marrying them, and two girls,
sisters, discussing a rich suitor whom they had just been
kissing, say the following: The Elder Sister: "Well it's all
the same to you because nothing is going to come of it, but

he's going to marry me." The Younger Sister: "I'm not thinking about anything of the sort." The Older Sister: "If you like him for himself, then you can take him away from me after the wedding. It won't bother me at all. I'll have an Uhlan with a black mustache for a house friend." Since the entire play is written in the same spirit, then I assume, of course, that it is not fitting for presentation on the stage.[30]

Because of censorship Briusov was not successful in this attempt to give the bourgeosie a slap in the face; but in the following year, with the appearance of *The Russian Symbolists (Russkie simvolisty),* he was to succeed in gaining a notoriety greater than he had ever imagined or even dared to hope for.

CHAPTER TWO

Elusive Fame (1894-1898)

1. The Birth of the Movement: "The Russian Symbolists" (1894-1895)

In the first week of March, 1894, exactly one year after he had predicted that he would be the leader of a future Russian Symbolist movement, Briusov, in collaboration with an old companion from Kreiman's Gymnasium, A. A. Lang (under the pseudonym A. Miropolsky), published the first installment (*vypusk*) of *The Russian Symbolists (Russkie simvolisty)*. Discussing the anthologies in retrospect, Briusov wrote:

... I attempted to give *models* of all forms of the "new poetry," with which I myself had managed to become acquainted: vers libre, lexical instrumentation, Parnassian clearness, intentional obscuring of sense in the spirit of Mallarmé, the youthful familiarity of Rimbaud, the dandyism of rare words in the manner of Laurent Tailhade, and so on right up to my "famous" single-line poem ["O cover thy pale legs!"] , and along with this—translated models of all the most prominent French Symbolists. Whoever wants to re-examine the two thin little installments of *The Russian Symbolists* will, of course, see in them this conscious selection of *models*, which made them into a sort of small anthology.[1]

Fortunately for Briusov, and perhaps for Russian Symbolism in general, Vladimir Solovyov, the highly respected Russian philosopher, poet, and critic, did not regard *The Russian Symbolists* as a mere anthology, Solovyov's devastatingly sarcastic reviews in *The Messenger of Europe*[2] were most likely the single most important criticism ever received by Briusov or tne Symbolists for bringing attention to the new movement. In his first review, after noting certain obvious parodies of

Fet, Solovyov wrote his famous interpretation of the following Briusov poem:

> Golden fairies
> In a satin garden!
> When shall I find
> The glacial avenues?
>
> The silvery splashes
> Of amorous naiads!
> Where the jealous planks
> Bar the way to you?
>
> Incomprehensible bowls
> Illuminated by fire,
> The dawn is stultified
> Over the flight of fantasies.
>
> Beyond the dark of veils
> Are funeral urns,
> And the azure vault
> Does not await the deceptive stars.[3]

In spite of the glacial avenues in a satin garden," the plot of this poem is as clear as it is reprehensible. Carried away by "a flight of fantasies," the author has become lost in the contemplation of fenced baths where persons of the female sex, whom he calls "fairies" and "naiads," are bathing. But can one expiate villainous actions with splendid words?... Let us hope at least that the "jealous planks" prove to be up to their calling. In the event this is not the case, then all that would be left for the "golden fairies" to do would be to douse the immodest Symbolist from those "incomprehensible bowls" which in the colloquial language are called washtubs and are used in the baths for the ablution of feet.[4]

As far as the young poet himself was concerned, Solovyov's prognosis was not favorable: "It is not possible to make a general judgment concerning Mr. Valery Briusov not knowing his age. If he is no older than fourteen then he might turn into a decent poet, and perhaps into nothing. But if he is a grown

Valery Briusov

man, then, of course, any literary hopes are out of
place" (p. 892).

A review written under the pseudonym of Ivan-
ushka Durachok in *New Times (Novoe Vremia)*
was kinder to Briusov personally, although just as
derisive in regard to "the Symbolists" and the book
itself. Noting that in the "little book about how
not to write poetry" there were nevertheless "two
or three sonorous, nice little poems *[stikhotvoren'-
itsa]*," Durachok says that Briusov, a man "not without a little talent *[ne bez darovanitsa]*," has spoiled
the joking tone of the collection and advises him
"to discard the 'satin gardens' and 'jealous' planks'
and to leave the profane mob, or, if not, then to
maintain the tone and dress up in his fool's costume
forever."[5]

Briusov was exhilarated by the criticism, and
in his diary he exclaimed: "I feel myself a true poet!"
(p. 16). This was the beginning. Now Briusov prepared for the second collection with renewed vigor
and enthusiasm. In June, 1894, he wrote Lang:
"Our [second] collection must be both beautiful
and symbolic. All that we have must be turned into
chefs d'oeuvres. If necessary, we will write everything new! Forward! I am compiling the collection
with dictatorial power."[6] And indeed, the response
to the first anthology of *The Russian Symbolists* was
mild in comparison to the roars of outrage provoked
by the publication of the second installment some
seven months later. The book, said its critics, displayed the "weakness of home-grown originality"
(Universal Illustrated [Vsemirnaia illiustratsia]); it
was described as a "fantastic collection liberated
from the censorship of common sense" *(The Week
[Nedelia])*; an example of "untalented people
placing their absurd hope on the ... future" *(Russian Wealth);* and "a war against common sense,
announced by untalented dullards, among whom
only V. Briusov offers some hope as a versifier"

The Observer (Nabliudatel'). The collection exhibited a "lack of content, a perversion of language" with "only a few poems by Briusov nice, gracious, and not without content" *(Russian Review).*[7] But Vladimir Solovyov, again writing in *The Messenger of Europe,* still had no kind words for Briusov. He began by noting the incredible facility with which the number of the Symbolists increased *("generatio aequivoca")*—"in the summer they were only two, but now they are already an entire ten"; he could not have known, of course, that Briusov was writing under at least five different pseudonyms to create precisely this impression. Solovyov then once again turned to the fledgling poet:

Mr. V. Briusov, the same one who, in the first installment of *The Russian Symbolists,* described his reprehensible peeking into the ladies' baths, now depicts his own bath. This, of course, is no misfortune; but what is bad is that Briusov speaks about his bathing in such words that clearly show, not merely hint at, the author's not entirely normal condition. We warned him that pandering to base passions, even be it under the guise of Symbolism, would lead to no good. Alas, our premonitions were realized earlier than expected. Judge for yourself:

> In the silver dust the midnight damp
> Makes tired dreams the prisoners of rest,
> And in the *unsteady silence of the river's sarcophagus*
> *A great man hears not slander.*

To call a river a sarcophagus and one's own self a great man is an entirely clear sign (and not merely a hint) of a diseased condition.[8]

With the appearance of the third installment of *The Russian Symbolists* even Mikhailovsky felt called upon to reprove the brash newcomer, and he expressed the hope that perhaps one day Briusov would experience "a brightening of his intellect and become ashamed of his present stupidities."[9] Of all Briusov's

"stupidities," the one that received the most notoriety was his one-line poem, "Oh, cover thy pale
legs!" Vladimir Solovyov treated it humorously,
saying that it was the most perfect poem ever written by Briusov and could be made even more perfect
by the addition of "for otherwise thou willst catch
cold," but, he continued, "even without that, Mr.
Briusov's advice, evidently addressed to a creature
suffering from anemia, is the most meaningful work
of all Symbolist literature, not only Russian, but
foreign as well."[10] P. F. Yakubovich, writing in
Russian Wealth, was of a different mind: "Briusov's
one line poem about 'pale legs' did more harm to
the Decadents than all the critics' reviews put together."[11] This was hardly the case. A more considered statement would be that Briusov's one-line
poem did more than all the critic's reviews put together (with the exception of Solovyov's) to establish
the young poet as the acknowledged leader of the
still non-existent Symbolist movement.

Now, sixty-five years later, it is difficult to ap-
preciate the indignation aroused by Briusov's line.
The critics were not disturbed by the "meaning,"
however, as much as they were by the form. This
radical departure from all accepted norms of poetry
caused greater shock on the part of the older generation than any implied meaning. As Yury Tynianov
points out, " 'Why one line?' was the first question
of the readers from *Russian Wealth* and *The Messenger of Europe* and 'What do these legs mean?' was only
the second question."[12]

By September 5, 1895, Briusov's dream was
realized. Writing in *News of the Day (Novosti dnia),*
I. Ya. Gurliand called Briusov "the chief Decadent"
and the "Decadent ringleader *[konovod]*."[13] It was
Briusov's patent mystifications, however, that led
the critics to talk about a "Decadent movement"
(at that time the terms "Decadent" and "Symbolist"
were still synonymous in Russia) when, in fact,

there was as yet no such thing. As Briusov relates the history of the movement's beginnings, it was not his work but the critics' imagination that catapulted him to the position of "ringleader." Even before his "coronation" by *News of the Day,* Briusov recognized that his fame—or better, notoriety—was growing rapidly. On December 15, 1894, he wrote in his diary:"...at the beginning of this notebook no one knew about me, but now, but now all the journals are cursing me. Today the *News of the Day* calmly writes 'Briusov' knowing that the name is known to its readers" (p. 20). He never deluded himself about the nature of his "fame," however, and explained it candidly in his "Autobiography":

If one morning I did not wake up "famous" as once did Byron, then in any case I was quickly made the wistful hero of the cheap newspapers and of the glib feuilleton writers who were unscrupulous in their topics.... They forcibly tied me to the role of leader of a new school, *maître de l'école* of a school of Russian Symbolists, which actually did not exist then at all.... Thus I turned out to be a leader without troops. It was necessary, however, *faire bonne mine à mauvais jeu.* They wanted to consider me none other than a Symbolist; I tried to become what they wanted me to be (p. 109).

To a certain extent this statement is doubtful if one takes into consideration Briusov's diary entry for March 4, 1893, in which he proclaims himself the future leader of Russian Symbolism. Moreover, the entries for 1894 and 1895 in his diaries leave no doubt but that Briusov was engaged in a conscious, deliberate effort to establish a "Symbolist school" in Russia. Particularly revealing in this light are Briusov's statements in an article which he wrote entitled "Interview on Symbolism" published in *News of the Day* on August 30, 1894, that is, shortly after the publication of the first installment of *The Russian Symbolists.*[14]

It is of special interest that even at this early

Valery Briusov

date Briusov was already cognizant of the existence
of *two* incipient Symbolist schools, one in Moscow,
the other in St. Petersburg: "As French Symbolism
divided into different schools (instrumentalists, magicians, etc.), so too among us a split is taking place,
to be sure not a desired one. An entirely separate
circle of Petersburg Symbolists has already split off;
yes, and even among us, among the participants in
The Russian Symbolists, one rarely finds identical
opinions."[15] At this point Briusov spells out the
difference between the Petersburg and Moscow
groups: "The theory expounded in your article has
been chiefly disseminated in the Petersburg circle
where personal claim is laid to it by a certain A.
Dobroliubov, who is preparing a large work on Symbolism. The majority of us [that is, in Moscow] ad-
here to the view of Symbolism as a poetry of nuances,
in contra-distinction to the previous poetry of
colors. "Nous voulons de la nuance, pas la couleur,
rien que la nuance!" as Verlaine says. "Peculiarity of
content summons forth peculiarities in language"
(p. 268).[16]

Finally, Briusov announced to the world
through the pages of *News of the Day*—certainly a
broader audience than he had enjoyed with the first
installment of *The Russian Symbolists*—the pending
formation of the Symbolist school:

In any case, the uniting of the "Russian Symbolists" is our
next task. With this aim in mind we propose to disseminate
our collection and to educate society. Furthermore, an edition of the leading figures of French Symbolism in Russian
translation has been undertaken in order to make the models
more accessible. Thus Mr. M. (his verses will be in the second
installment) has taken up the translation of Mallarmé's *Pages*
and I have already finished and shall soon publish a full translation of Verlaine's *Romances sans Paroles* (p. 268).

After the publication of *The Russian Symbolists* and Briusov's translation of *Romances sans*

Paroles in 1894, Symbolist and would-be Symbolist
poets from all over Russia and even from Europe
began contacting the young poet, editor, and translator in person and by post. Aleksandr Dobroliubov,
the "arch Symbolist," and V. Gippius came from St.
Petersburg and spent several days with Briusov discussing poetry and the movement; he received letters
from Louise Bourgoin, whose poems he had translated for inclusion in the second installment; and he
met the young Symbolist poet Martov (pseudonym
for A. Bugon), who offered his work for eventual
publication in *The Russian Symbolists*. Briusov's
long friendship and correspondence with P. P. Pertsov,
the well-known literary figure of the era (and editor
from 1903-1904 of *The New Way [Novyi put']*),
also dates from this period.[17]
   Although the work of Merezhkovsky and
Minsky—to name but two—was a departure from
the tenets of contemporary Russian literature, it
was lacking in any sustaining force. Merezhkovsky's
direction was split between his Decadence, his God-
seeking, his mythology, and his struggles with the
Antichrist. Minsky, on the other hand, although he
often produced interesting content, was a second-
rate poet of the Nadsonian school who eventually
returned to "civic" themes.[18] The publications of
these two men as well as those of other Modernists
during the years 1884-1894 notwithstanding, the
three installments of *The Russian Symbolists*
marked a turning point in the history of Symbolism
in Russia:

The Russian Symbolists achieved what we desired—they fulfilled our cause. Our anthologies served the new in poetry, in
whatever forms this new might have been expressed. *In
tyrannos*, that is what our banner was. We were reproached—
too often even by our friends—for devoting too much space
to the new school's extremes. Even granting that these extremes will pass as a consequence of poetry's renewal, we
dare to think that in the days of the struggle they would

have only the most beneficial influence. Stop before nothing!
Dare everything! That is our motto.[19]

Unlike Mikhailovsky, those critics who had no
particular axe to grind were intrigued by this new
phenomenon in Russian poetry. The hitherto alien
devotion to form, the riot of barbarisms, the daz-
zling synaesthesia (borrowed from Poe and Baudelaire), the profusion of sonorous sound repetitions—
not for some plebeian onomatopoeic purpose but
for the sake of the sounds themselves—and, above
all, the philosophy of the thought unspoken, the
desire, in Briusov's expression, "to hypnotize the
reader" and to "create a certain mood in him," the
desire to elevate the individual in an age where the
law was denial of self; all of these served to over-
whelm the critics and the reading public. The impact of the "new ideas," particularly as expressed
by Briusov and Balmont, has been likened by one
critic, not without justification, to the impact of
the *Sturm und Drang* period on German literature.[20]
It is safe to say that after the publication of
The Russian Symbolists and the translation of
Romances sans Paroles—the products solely of
Briusov's ingenuity and daring—and Balmont's *Under
Northern Skies (Pod severnym nebom)*, 1894, the
course of Russian literature, essentially monolithic
for the preceding fifty years, was changed forever.

It was inevitable, of course, that Briusov and
Balmont meet. The story of their friendship is an
interesting sidelight in the history of the growth of
Symbolism in Russia; it also deserves mention for
the effect it had on Briusov's career. Briusov first
met Konstantin Balmont on September 28, 1894,
when he and Lang joined the Society of Lovers of
Western Literature *(Obshchestvo liubitelei zapadnoi
literatury)*. In the following months he and Balmont
spent most of their time together, discussing poetry,
the movement, and, more often than not, indulging

in heavy drinking bouts lasting the entire night.
(Dnevniki, pp. 19-20.) The relationship was a profitable one for Briusov, and he subsequently con-
fessed his indebtedness to Balmont in his "Autobiography": "[Balmont's] ecstatic love for poetry,
his subtle feeling for poetic beauty, his peculiar personality, made an extraordinary impression on me.
A great deal, a very great deal became comprehen-
sible for me and was disclosed to me only through
Balmont. He taught me how to understand other
poets, he taught me how to love life truly. I mean
that he unveiled in my soul that which was slum-
bering there and which, without his influence,
might have long continued to slumber.... I was one
way before my meeting with Balmont and became
another after my acquaintance with him" (p. 111).
The friendship between these two young men—
whom Renato Poggioli called the most significant
representatives of the Decadent movement in
Russia[21]—was a stormy and complex one, mostly
because of Briusov's personal doubts and his ambiguous feelings toward his older friend. During the
years from 1894-1900 Briusov's self-confidence in
his future greatness constantly fluctuated, descending
from the heights of exalted assurance to the depths
of bleak depression. Balmont, however, seldom if
ever wavered in his conviction that he was the
greatest innovator Russian poetry had ever known.
Balmont's *joie de vivre* often had an adverse effect
on Briusov's moods. For example, on November
19, 1897, Briusov entered into his diary: "Balmont
has arrived, he whom I have so long awaited.... it
was the same as two years ago, as though I was my
former self, the confident poet. When I began to read
my poems [to him] I became ashamed, not of the
poems—they were good—but that they were so few...
His life is now brighter than before, and mine is losing
its luster" (pp. 30-31).

It must have seemed to Briusov that his career,

so promising at twenty-one, was drawing to a close
at twenty-three. After the furor caused by *The
Russian Symbolists* in 1894 and 1895, Briusov's
next two collections of poems, *Chefs d'Oeuvre
(Shedevry),* in 1895 and *This is I (Me eum esse)* in
1896, brought him, with few exceptions, nothing
but scorn and ridicule from the critics and led to his
virtual banishment from the ranks of Russian literature.

2. Literary Excommunication (1895-1898)

From March to August, 1895, Briusov devoted
all his considerable energy to one task, the preparation and publication of his first independent collection of poems, *Chefs d'Oeuvre.* His letters and memoirs reveal that he had serious doubts about the re-
ception of this little book. Thus, on August 25, 1895,
a few days after the book's publication, he wrote to
P. P. Pertsov:

There were moments when I considered simply throwing all
copies of it into the fire. "What kind of *Chefs d'Oeuvre* are
these," I would say to myself, "pathetic doggerels with pre-
tensions and that is all." But in the end result—as always
happens—my dumb instincts prevailed. I convinced my feelings, which were firm, that even if *Chefs d'Oeuvre* were not
chefs d'oeuvre they were still better than my previously
printed poems, better than many poems of contemporary
poets, etc. I, of course, did not believe this, but I pretended
I did; and so I sit and with some kind of spite I send out my
little books.[22]

And after the book appeared, Briusov's worst fears
were realized. Once again it was not so much the
content of the book—for reviews barely mentioned
the content—as it was the audacity of the "Introduction" that incensed the critics. The "Introduction" is a classic example of baiting the bourgeoisie:

Chefs d'Oeuvre is the last book of my youth; its name has its own story, but it never meant "the *chefs d'oeuvre* of my poetry," because in the future I shall write much more significant things (it is permissible to make promises at 21!). Printing my book in our time I do not expect a fair evaluation for it from the critics or from the public. Not to my contemporaries and not even to mankind do I dedicate my book, but to eternity and art.[23]

The critics reacted immediately. They asserted that Briusov was mentally ill, had "delusions of grandeur," or was pretending to be sick so that he might take liberties usually denied normal people. The poet was not at all immune, however, to the abuse being heaped upon him by the critics, and he wrote of his torment in his diary. Even worse than the critics' abuse was the censure suffered by the young Decadent at the hands of his friends: "August 30: My *Chefs d'Oeuvre* made, I confess, the worst impression on my friends. They do not voice their censure, but remain silent; that is even worse. September 1: I was so dumbfounded by my friends' polite silence about *Chefs d'Oeuvre* that I ran away yesterday to Kursinsky's."[24]

The invective hurled at Briusov was doubly insulting. Although his "Introduction" was obviously a calculated pose, his poetry—at least as far as he was concerned—was art. The fact that the critics apparently did not even bother to read it crushed him. Several years later Briusov continued to insist that the poems were artistically quite respectable: "As best as I can now judge my poems myself [1913], there were no *'chefs d'oeuvre'* in the book, but there were good poems, some *very* good, and the majority was quite satisfactory. There were not more than two or three thoroughly bad ones. The critics, however, read only the book's title, that is, they only remembered the title and the noise surrounding my name quadrupled."[25] As a result of this "noise," Briusov became more firmly established as

Valery Briusov

Russia's foremost Decadent poet, but even more completely isolated from the world of Russian letters: "I
was publicly sentenced to 'excommunication from
literature,' and all journals became closed to me
for many years, approximately... five."[26]
    At this time the only way to remain in the
public eye was to publish in the various monthly
journals. Of course, it was possible to publish one's
own books—as Briusov was to do with the second
edition of *Chefs d'Oeuvre* and with *This is I* in 1896—
but books were a losing proposition financially, and
even more important for Briusov, critically as well.[27]
In the face of the extremely adverse reaction to
Chefs d'Oeuvre, it is only further testimony to the
strength of Briusov's determination and the force of
his ambition that in December, 1895, he issued a
second edition of the ill-fated book (which, however,
has 1896 as the date of publication). In his "Introduction" he not only refused to make any concessions
to prevailing sentiment, he reaffirmed his previous
position with intensified conviction and with some
additional caustic comments about the "lack of understanding" and the pathetic level of poetic appreciation in Russia: "I no longer find it necessary to
conceal, because of minor shortcomings, any works
in which parts are outstanding, especially because in
spirit and style they quite belong to *Chefs d'Oeuvre.*
Let there sound in full strength that chorus, the
voices of which are traveling into the far future. In
its present form my book appears to me to be
fully finished; and more calmly than ever, I dedicate
it to eternity, because a work of poetry cannot die.
Everything in the world is transitory except works
of art."[28] But for all his determination and feigned
self-confidence, Briusov was unable to change
public opinion, and entries in his diary continue to
reflect the poet's bitterness: "December 17: I have
just put *Chefs d'Oeuvre* [2nd edition] on the market, but being sick I wrote worse than I could have,

[43]

being poor I printed it worse than I would have liked. Everyone has renounced my book, even my friends. It is bitter. December 20: I notice that the failure of *Chefs d'Oeuvre* has, to a large degree, robbed my self-assurance, and at one time it was totally sincere! What a pity" (p. 23).

With the coming of the new year, 1897, Briusov once again rallied his flagging spirits and made yet another attempt to step into the literary limelight with the publication of his new collection of poems, *This is I,* meant to be "a huge mockery of the entire human race" with "not one sensible word in it" *(Dnevniki,* p. 23). It was to no avail. He not only failed to achieve his desired goal with *This is I,* the work also failed to evoke the critical abuse and sensationalism that had attended his earlier publications. The years 1896 and 1897 mark the lowest point in Briusov's literary fortunes and signal his greatest personal disillusionment and despondency. To defend himself from the wreckage of his world, Briusov vowed in his diary in November, 1896 to refrain from all literary activity for two years: "I shall read only what is great, write only in those minutes when I shall have something to tell the whole world.... I shall allow my fantasy, my pride, and my ego to sleep." This by no means implied, however, that the poet was surrendering, for he continues: "But this sleep will be more apparent than real. Thus a tiger closes his eyes in order to track his victim more surely. And my prey is already foredoomed. I am coming. Trumpets sound!" (p. 26).

It is solely from Briusov's diaries that we may judge the loneliness and despondency he suffered during these bleak years. His only friends, Balmont, Kursinsky, and Samygin were mostly out of town or abroad; life at the university was discouraging because of his lagging studies. Interestingly enough, it was in 1897 when Briusov elected—and the word

is used advisedly—his bride, Ioanna Matveevna
Frunt. There are but two rather brief, uninspired
entries in his diary that even mention his approach-
ing marriage. The marriage took place in September
of that same year. As it turned out, Briusov elected
wisely, for in spite of his many future infidelities,
his odd, irregular moods, and his strict, gloomy disposition and severity, Ioanna Matveevna never left
him and subordinated her will to his, serving until
his death as his secretary, sounding board, scape-
goat, and companion. After Briusov's death she
spent the remainder of her life editing and publishing from Briusov's archives to ensure that, as he
desired, "two lines in world literary history" would
be written about him.[29]

From 1896 through 1899, that is both before
and after his marriage, Briusov undertook a series
of journeys to help alleviate his boredom and dis-
appointment. He traveled often to St. Petersburg,
visited Riga, Warsaw, and the Crimea several times,
as well as the Caucasus. Although these journeys
generally provided occasional distraction, they offered him little consolation. Not even the magnificent vistas offered by the Caucasus were able to
make Briusov forget the feeling of failure that was
constantly gnawing at him.

The one journey abroad that excited Briusov
was to Germany. He was enthralled by the art
treasures in the museums of Berlin, and his imagination was captivated by the "splendor" of the
medieval "temples" of Cologne and Aachen. It
was during his stay in these cities that he thought
for the first time about the theme of his future
novel *Fiery Angel.*[30]

Undoubtedly the sudden impulse to travel
came in part from Briusov's desire to keep his vow
of abstinence from literature. It is clear that he hardly expected to be able to abide by his decision, and
he was right. By March, 1897, he was as deeply

involved with literature as he had ever been:

> What am I occupied with now? Right now: the "Introduction" to my *History of Lyrical Poetry;* a report on Rousseau for Gere [a professor at the university] ; a report for Kliuchevsky (alas! it is obligatory); my Symbolist drama; an epic about Rousseau; a novel *This is History;* a tale about Helen; my translation of the *Aeneid;* a little epic about Moscow; a monograph *Nero: Legion and Phalanx.* Already conceived: a drama, *Marina Mnishek; Atlantis;* a translation of Maeterlinck's *Les Trésors,* a story, *The Exiles.* In the future: *History of Roman Literature; History of the Emperors; History of Scholasticism;* a public lecture on Rimbaud. I am reading: Weber, Maeterlinck, the Bible, and Sumarokov. I must read: Kant, Novalis, and Boileau.[31]

It is quite characteristic that there are as many references to pure scholarship in the above passage as there are to pure literary activity. The two were inseparable for Briusov, and with his passionate dedication to learning, it is not surprising that he was to become—in the words of Maxim Gorky as well as others—"the most cultured man in Russia."[32] Briusov was aware that his scholarship might have an adverse effect on his poetry, and on January 29, 1898, he wrote in his diary: "The study of philosophy somehow kills poetry. Poetry requires a certain naiveté of thought. The mind, experienced in metaphysical refinements, rejects the approximateness of poetic language" (p. 33). But it was this mixture of the "refinements" of scholarship and the "approximateness" of poetic language that became the most distinguishing feature of Briusov's poetry. By the same token, it was this same erudition that frequently served to provide his more biased critics with additional ammunition in their attacks on his work (while, ironically enough, they praise Mandelstam for precisely this same propensity).

The many setbacks suffered by Briusov during

Valery Briusov

these years as well as his "withdrawal from literary
life" with its peculiarly intense expression are reflected in one of his first metapoetical verses, "To
the Young Poet," written in 1896 and included in
the first edition of *This is I.*

> Pale youth with burning gaze,
> I give unto thee three commandments now:
> Accept the first: do not live in the present,
> Only the future is the poet's realm.
>
> Remember the second: sympathize with no man,
> But love only thyself, boundlessly.
> Keep the third: worship art alone,
> It alone, without reflection, without goal.
>
> Pale youth with confused gaze,
> If you accept my three commandments,
> Silently shall I fall, a conquered warrior,
> Knowing that I shall leave a poet in the world.[33]

This egocentric, strangely passionless, yet nevertheless fierce stance is quite in keeping with the development of the poet's personality as we have thus
far observed it, and Briusov was to remain consistent
in his self-imposed isolation as he indeed remained
consistent in his attitudes toward life in general. This
becomes eminently clear when the above poem is
compared with his often quoted verse "To the Poet,"
written in 1907 and included in *All the Melodies*
when his career was at the apogee of its spectacular
rise.

> You must be proud as a banner;
> You must be sharp as a sword;
> As with Dante, the subterranian flame
> Must scorch your cheeks.
>
> Be a cold witness to everything,
> Upon everything directing your gaze.

Let your virtue be
A readiness to walk onto the pyre.

Perhaps everything in life is but material
For brightly singing verse,
And you, from your carefree childhood
Seek combinations of words.

In the minutes of passion's embraces
Force yourself to be passionless,
And in the hour of merciless crucifixion
Glorify your frenzied pain.

In the morning's dreams and in the evening's abyss
Harken unto that which Fate whispers to you,
And remember: for all time, of thorns
Has been made the poet's cherished crown.[34]

As a concomitant to his increasing reliance on
his own personality and talent—perhaps to bolster
his lagging self-esteem—Briusov gradually became
disillusioned with and rejected the few friends he
had made during the last few years. It is not un-
likely that he simply decided that the effort involved in being what he called "my former self,"
that is to say the obnoxious, devil-may-care, young
Decadent he was at the time of his initial friendship
with A. Dobroliubov and Balmont, was simply not
worth it. In three consecutive entries made in July,
1898 he expresses his new-found dissatisfaction
with Kursinsky, Dobroliubov, and Samygin. His
references to Balmont continue to display their
former love-hate tendencies, with hate rapidly
gaining the upper hand.[35]
Perhaps his prolonged isolation and despondency simply became unbearable, perhaps his ego
no longer could endure the blows it was suffering
from his probing, introspective insights, perhaps
it was the thrill of again completing a work for
publication, or perhaps it was another prophetic

vision, but whatever the case, on writing the last
lines of his little book *On Art (O iskusstve),* Briusov
found renewed inspiration and self-confidence. The
feeling that he was "obligated" to fulfill his poten-
tial, to "conquer," and to live up to his "youth of a
genius" was steadily mounting.[36] He again discovered within him the means to rise to his destiny:

I have finished my book on art. Here it lies before me.
Blessed is the resurrected pride of the creator! Great is the
mystery of words and of their powers. Some are almost like
silver trumpets in the field, others are created by angels,
others are immobility and death itself. Happy is he who knows
the incantation. On his signal the harmonious host gathers
in disarray. Oh, triumph of the conquerors, going with un-
furled banners! Audible are the cries of the warriors, the
singing of the horns. Blessed is the resurrected pride of the
leader.[37]

And the leader's resurrected pride soon enabled him
to resurrect his career, for it was not long after this
that Briusov returned from his banishment to assume what he considered to be his rightful position
in Russian literature.

CHAPTER THREE

The Leader Emerges (1898-1904)

1. "A bright year in my life!" (1898-1899)

Briusov has said that beginning with 1898 his biography and his bibliography merge into one,[1] and indeed from this point on he was totally wedded to literature. With his renewed determination "to advance," he once more attempted to publish in one of the leading Russian journals, this time not as a brash decadent but as a serious literary scholar. In September he took an article on Tiutchev to the offices of *Russian Archive (Russkii arkhiv)* where he met P. Bartenev, the grand old man of Russian journalism. They spoke at length, mostly about Tiutchev, Baratynsky, and Pushkin (Bartenev was one of Russia's first Pushkinists). The old man must have been impressed with Briusov's erudition and knowledge of Russian literature, for not only did he accept and publish the young poet's article, "On F. I. Tiutchev's Collected Works," but he also commissioned Briusov to translate several of Tiutchev's letters for publication in *Russian Archive.* The ultimate mark of Bartenev's respect for Briusov as a scholar, however, came in October of the same year when Bartenev requested that the poet correct the proofs of a new Tiutchev edition being published by Bartenev. Undoubtedly the old man's good will was in no small way responsible for the many new publishing outlets that were rapidly opened to Briusov.

Of course, it was not merely the fact that Briusov went to *Russian Archive* with an article on Tiutchev rather than Maeterlinck and with talk of Russia's Golden Age rather than of France's Decadence which won over the conservative Bartenev. Briusov had not returned from his literary Coventry

without some new insights and maturity, and it was
by design that he concealed his previously insulting
manner and his unbridled conceit. But what seemed
perhaps modest to Briusov was not necessarily so
in the opinion of others. Thus, although Briusov
had changed the "Introduction" to his little book,
On Art, before its publication to make it appear
"more modest,"[2] it nevertheless contained many
characteristic Briusovisms such as "both Tolstoy
and I."

In spite of these favorable turns in his fortune,
Briusov felt alone in Moscow. Most of the nation's
literary activity was taking place in St. Petersburg,
and although the "Moscow Decadents" had for a
time captured the literary limelight with *The Russian
Symbolists,* nothing much had happened in Moscow
since Briusov had been silenced. Even though self-
reliance was one of the poet's most dominant character traits, he still possessed the human need to
have someone with whom he could discuss his work.
The one who best fulfilled this need for Briusov
was Balmont, but Balmont now rarely spent much
time in Moscow. So in December, 1898 in search of
companionship and inspiration, Briusov spent nine
days in St. Petersburg where he once again immersed
himself in the frenzied activity of the "new ideas."
The descriptions in Briusov's diary of these days in
the capital, although brief, constitute one of the most
informative and interesting accounts of Russian
literary society at the end of the century. His por-
trayal of Sluchevsky's famous "Fridays" is revealing for its penetrating insights into the petty jeal-
ousies and rivalries in which so many struggling
literary figures were involved. While in St. Petersburg, Briusov met such prominent figures as Merezhkovsky and his wife the poetess Zinaida Gippius,
Minsky, Sologub, Bunin, V. Gippius, Sokolov, Yasinsky, and Sluchevsky. An interesting sidelight to
Briusov's visit was provided by his first meeting with

Valery Briusov

Zinaida Gippius, a meeting that resulted in their future enmity. After reading Briusov's account of the meeting, one can hardly be surprised that their relations later were strained. "[Balmont and I] went to see Merezhkovsky who was ill. At first Zinaida Gippius served us tea in a dark, dirty dining room. She did not attempt to be kind, and little by little began to be fresh to me. I paid her back in kind and know that two or three of my blows were well aimed. Thus, when she was deriding [Aleksandr] Dobroliubov I said with the most unassuming look, 'And do you know, it seemed to me that you imitate him in your poems'." (*Dnevniki,* p. 53).

While in St. Petersburg Briusov also met a young and unknown poet who evidently impressed him more than anyone else writing at the time: Ivan Ivanovich Oreus, who wrote under the name of Ivan Konevskoy. After having listened to V. Gippius, Minsky, Korinfsky, Lebedev, and others read their poetry at Sologub's one evening, Briusov wrote in his diary that Oreus' reading was "the most remarkable, for he is an excellent poet" (p. 57). This was unusual praise for a contemporary from the pen of Briusov. Although he and Oreus did not get along well at their first meeting, Briusov's respect for the young man's talent never diminished. Eventually Briusov wrote the introduction and edited a posthumous edition of the works of Oreus, who died in 1901 at the age of twenty-four.

Upon returning to Moscow, Briusov could not help feeling pleased and excited with his new good fortune, and for the first time in many years he greeted the approach of a new year with high spirits as the following diary entry attests: "I must take my farewell of the old [year]; for me it was quite a good one, and I can review it only with gratitude. It was a very bright year in my life! The Crimea, my article about art, my meeting with Dobroliubov, my articles on Tiutchev, my trip to St. Petersburg, and many

good poems—all this may be mentioned. I do not
know what kind of year the new one will be with
such a gloomy name as 'ninety-nine' " (p. 59). The
answer was to be "an even better year than last,"
for 1899 was the year in which Briusov was gradu-
ated from the university and the first year in which
he was able to devote himself solely to literature
and to his pursuit of greatness. His "successes" began to multiply rapidly. Although he was not nearly
as well prepared as he might have been, in April and
May, 1899, Briusov passed his comprehensive examinations at the university with no difficulty.

In March he had made a second trip to St.
Petersburg where he managed to establish firmer relations with the leading figures of Russian literary
society and to impress these new acquaintances with
his erudition and poetic prowess—the hypercritical
Merezhkovsky was moved to exclaim "it has some
original images!" when he heard Briusov read his
"Demons of Dust" *(Dnevniki,* p. 65). His greatest
practical success, however, came when Bunin printed
some of Briusov's poems in *The Southern Review
(Yuzhnoe obozrenie),* for these were practically the
first of his poems to appear in print which were not
published himself. By July he was so overwhelmed
by the excellent state of his affairs that, comparing himself to Polycrates—an unflattering but perhaps
telling choice, he wrote in his diary: "...I am fright-
ened by the surplus of my good fortune. Where is
the prayer in order to preserve it longer, in order
that the gods *comiter conservent* my bliss. I stand
in horror before the morrow. But today let a prayer
be my last word: I am thankful!" (p. 74).

2. Preparing to Lead: The Founding of "Skorpion" (1899-1904)

Briusov continued to work at *Russian Archive,*
learning the rudiments of publishing, editing, and

bibliography under the guidance of Bartenev. It was
also at *Russian Archive* that Briusov gained the astute
business sense that was to stand him in such good
stead in the future. For the first time in his life he
was working at a full-time job. In the beginning it
was more a labor of love—and, of course, of opportunity, but later, in August, 1900, Briusov officially
became Bartenev's employee. He continued in the
position of "secretary" of the journal for three
years, and his duties, according to a contract he
drew up, were to "include everything having to do
with the publication of *Russian Archive,* such as:
reading proofs, writing business letters, dealing with
booksellers and printers, etc."[3] Briusov's scholarly
inclinations were able to blossom now that the
journal's archives were accessible to him. It was here
that his interest in collecting, editing, and publishing
manuscripts grew into a lifelong passion. At *Russian
Archive* he learned much about the editing and
publishing of "collected works." His first ventures
into Pushkiniana came as a result of his close association with Bartenev when in 1899 he published
"What does an academic edition of Pushkin's works
offer?" the first in a long series of publications on
Pushkin.[4]

With all the encouraging signs of acceptance,
Briusov again ventured to publish some of his own
poems, this time in a collection entitled *Book of
Meditations (Kniga razdumii),* which contained
poems by him, Balmont, Konevskoy, and Durnov.
The reviews, as usual, were not good, but for the
first time this did not throw Briusov into depression.
There are several reasons why he does not seem to
have been too concerned with the public's reaction
to his latest publication: he was quite occupied with
his editorial activities; he was working on his next
collection of poems, *Tertia Vigilia;* and, most significantly, he had changed his attitude toward his own
work and now claimed to be totally indifferent to

public opinion:

I can not write an insignificant work. Whatever I may write...
I will be a powerful creator. I will be able and must say everything with which my heart is full.... Now I have truly attained
that which I have asserted from childhood. Sincerely, to the
depths of my soul, I do not need readers, I need no salutes.
It is all the same to me. Do you understand the freedom
afforded by such a realization? Freedom, not from enemies,
that is easy, but from friends and those close to me. If before
I was not embarrassed by mockery, then now I am not de-
ceived, as I was, not too long ago, by the raptures [of others].
I even want to laugh at my admirers.[5]

This attitude, as will be seen, hardly obtained for
any extended period of time, but during these years
of intense literary activity—chiefly journalistic—
Briusov was indeed more concerned with creating his
school than he was with his image as a poet among
the critics, although his image as a poet among the
young Symbolist poets was, of course, always important to him. He soon recognized that if his
school was to be successful it would be necessary
to establish an outlet for its publications.
     Although he never hesitated to lavish praise
upon Balmont as a poet—and indeed as a poet who
had significantly influenced his work—Briusov failed
to acknowledge his indebtedness to Balmont for in-
troducing him into the most prominent Russian literary circles of the time. Undoubtedly the most important introduction ever extended him came in
July or August, 1899, when Balmont visited Briusov
with S. A. Poliakov and Yu. Baltrushaitis.
     Poliakov came from a wealthy family and was
a translator. He is chiefly known, however, as the
"most enlightened" Maecenas in Moscow.[6] It was
his money that enabled the Moscow Symbolists to
found the publishing house "Skorpion," and without "Skorpion" Russian Symbolism might never
have attained its dominant position in modern

Valery Briusov

Russian literature. G. Chulkov correctly notes that "were it not for [both Poliakov and "Skorpion"], Briusov's road would have been a rocky one."[7] For Briusov is not preeminent in Russian literature because of his poetry, although he would have gone down in Russian literary history as a leading Symbolist poet. He is truly significant because he organized a school from a most disparate group of poets and became "the leader" of the Russian Symbolists, and he became the leader chiefly through his journalistic activities.

Exactly when the idea of creating a publishing house devoted entirely to the works of the embryonic new movement was first conceived is not known. It is apparent from the entries in Briusov's diaries, however, that after this first meeting in the summer of 1899, Briusov, Balmont, Baltrushaitis, and Poliakov continued to meet regularly to discuss and plan the founding of "Skorpion." "Skorpion" is above all associated in the minds of students of Russian literature with the publication of *The Scales (Vesy)*, the first Russian journal entirely devoted to the new movement. But before the publication of the first issue of that journal in 1904, "Skorpion" had already been committed to publish the works of many young Decadent writers, the majority of whom could publish in no other place. During the last week in March, 1900, "Skorpion" issued its first book, a collection of poems by Aleksandr Dobroliubov with introductions by Ivan Konevskoy and Valery Briusov. This was Briusov's first written contribution to "Skorpion."[8]

In its first two years of existence, "Skorpion" published translations of Ibsen, Knut Hamsun, D'Annunzio, and Schnitzler. Original works included the above-mentioned volume of Dobroliubov's poetry, Briusov's *Tertia Vigilia,* a collection of short stories by Merezhkovsky, and Bunin's collection of poems, *The Falling of the Leaves (Listopad).* And

this was only the beginning. Although a statement
of purpose written for "Skorpion's" catalogue in
1902 said that the publishing house was "non-de-
nominational" insofar as literary schools were concerned, no effort was made to conceal its favorite:
" 'Skorpion' devotes much space to the publication
of translations of those authors who serve the so-
called 'new art.' There has been so much idle talk
in our press concerning the notorious Symbolism
and Decadence that the time has come to give
readers an opportunity to form an independent
opinion about the new movements in literature."[9]

The appearance of "Skorpion" on the literary
scene, however, by no means meant that the critics
and the public had accepted Symbolism; the publishing house was but the first move in Briusov's
campaign which would require several more years
before it could be considered a success. As Chulkov,
a participant and eye-witness to the struggle, explains
it:

The serious and active work of the literary artists K. A. Balmont, Yu. K. Baltrushaitis, V. Ya. Briusov, and a few others
was taking place behind the wings of "Skorpion"; but on the
stage, for the public, these poets were still entertaining ec-
centrics. Such, apparently, is the fate of any school. A
period of time is required for the *poètes maudits* to turn
into academicians. For Briusov and his friends this period
of time ended approximately in 1907. But for the seven
years before this, "Skorpion's" collaborators were "the
talk of the town."[10]

From the day it was founded, Briusov assumed
a key role in every phase of "Skorpion's" activity,
and he, perhaps more than anyone else, was responsible for its future success. The first achievement of
"Skorpion" was to unite temporarily the Moscow
Decadents with the St. Petersburg "God-seekers,"
for at that time "Skorpion" was the only publishing
house in which both groups could publish. For a

time at least, the common involvement in "Skorpion" served as a basis for civil relations between
Briusov and the Merezhkovskys.[11]

In the third week of October, 1900, "Skorpion" published Briusov's third collection of poems,
Tertia Vigilia, the collection, which according to
Briusov first brought him recognition as a poet:
"For the first time, in the reviews of this book,
they regarded me as a poet and not as a 'rarity,'
and for the first time I read praise about myself in
print (by M. Gorky... I. Yasinsky, and others)."[12]
Chulkov relates that when *Tertia Vigilia* appeared
Briusov was virtually unknown except for his notorious one-line poem. Therefore, when Chulkov
read a report on the new book at V. A. Morozova's
famous literary salon, he created "a sensation."[13]
Word of Briusov's talents, however, had already
started to get around, due mostly to the efforts of
Bunin and Baltrushaitis, who were greatly impressed
with the young poet's abilities. Thus when Briusov
met Gorky for the first time in September, 1900,
the latter stated that he had long ago heard of Briusov, that he was interested in his work, that Bunin
had read him selections from *Tertia Vigilia,* and
that he had found them charming.[14]

The occasion for Briusov's meeting with
Gorky was the appearance of the first journal to be
published under the auspices of "Skorpion," *Northern Flowers (Severnye tsvety),* an annual literary
miscellany, the first issue of which appeared in
1901.[15] The creation of *Northern Flowers* is another
example of Briusov's ceaseless effort to build a
Symbolist movement. With the resources of "Skorpion" at his disposal and with the support of such
figures as Poliakov, Balmont, Baltrushaitis, and
Yasinsky, the time had finally come for Briusov to
achieve his long sought-after goal, and he set about
his business with passion and inexhaustible strength.
Bely remembers him at this time in the following

way:

...in 1900-1901 he would walk about Moscow with his little
notebook and his little pencil organizing young poets into a
literary party, drily setting the apparatus of the journals into
motion, teaching and scolding, inciting and pampering, and
always shedding, as a tree its leaves, a heap of strange cita-
tions from unknown poets of France, Belgium, England,
Czechoslovakia, Greece, Latvia, Poland, and Germany—
forging his battering ram with the stubbornness of a bull.[16]

Khodasevich remembers him in the 1900's in much
the same way:

He founded "Skorpion" and *The Scales* and ruled them with absolute power: he conducted polemics, concluded alliances,
declared wars, united and divided, made peace and quarrelled.
Manipulating many threads, both overt and covert, he
felt himself to be the captain of some great literary ship,
and he conducted his business with great vigilance. In addition to his natural inclination, he was impelled to wield
power by a consciousness of his own responsibility for the
ship's fate.[17]

   But it was not by his tireless activities alone
that he convinced—or even compelled—Russia's
leading poets to join the ranks of "Skorpion." Briusov had created a powerful physical image as well,
one which possessed an aura of mystery. Everyone
who ever met him and subsequently described the
meeting called attention to Briusov's invariable
frock coat, always buttoned to the top, and his
stance with arms folded upon his chest and head
raised at a haughty angle. Always speaking in a low,
constrained voice, he would astonish his listeners
with the most outrageous insult, and then, just as
suddenly, disarm them with an almost childlike
smile, displaying his brilliantly white teeth. His
dark figure, his high cheekbones, and his narrow,
almost Asiatic eyes reminded those who conversed

Valery Briusov

with him of the poet's favorite themes at the time—
sadism, voyeurism, masochism, necrophilia, and the
secrets of antiquity. Then, too, there were many
stories told about Briusov and about his interest in
the occult; these aided in creating an aura that hov-
ered about him even when he was engaged in the
most prosaic of business matters. The impression-
ability and easily excited imagination of young and
mystically oriented poets such as Bely and Blok did
much to disseminate this image of the maître as—in
Bely's phrase—"madness, tightly buttoned in a
frock coat."[18] Even if Chulkov's contention that
"Briusov's demonism was nothing more than a
literary mask" is correct, and it appears to be, it
hardly matters, for it achieved its aim.[19] His demonism and strange conduct in public almost hyp-
notized his followers into believing that he was
some sort of "black magician," possessed with
supernatural powers.[20] Briusov, of course, did
nothing to dispel these illusions.

By 1901 Briusov's endeavors were paying hand-
some dividends. The creation of "Skorpion," the
publication of *Tertia Vigilia*—more highly acclaimed
by his friends than anything else he had written—
the appearance of *Northern Flowers,* and his pose
as the movement's demonic maître all combined to
increase his exposure and heighten his influence.
"Skorpion's" success, it is true, was still modest, but
the publishing house appeared to have a promising
future, and Briusov was acknowledged to be in no
small measure responsible for its auspicious beginnings. His editorial and journalistic abilities were
greatly respected, as is evident when his role in the
founding of *The New Way* is examined.

The New Way had been the brain child of
Merezhkovsky and P. P. Pertsov as far back as 1895,[21]
but it was not until 1901 that the possibility of
publishing a journal in St. Petersburg dedicated to
the mystic, neo-Christian ideas of the capital's

Symbolists became feasible, and it was not until
1903 that the journal finally appeared. As already
mentioned, there was even at this early date some
friction between the Merezhkovskys and Briusov.
The Merezhkovskys were not so mystically oriented,
however, as to be blind to the inherent advantages
in enlisting Briusov's active support for their venture.
From 1901 to 1903 Briusov met frequently with
Merezhkovsky and his wife, Zinaida Gippius, both
in Moscow and in St. Petersburg. The Merezhkovskys' attitude toward the Moscow Decadent leader
became noticeably more cordial during this period.
Although Merezhkovsky and his followers realized
that Briusov would never be converted to their neo-
Christian ideas, they nevertheless invited him to become a secretary of their new journal.[22] Briusov,
who could hardly refuse this opportunity to publish
in another journal and at the same time gain a further foothold within the St. Petersburg group was
quick to agree. He had no delusions, however, about
the journal's chances for success. In November,
1902, he wrote Kornei Chukovsky: "a new journal
The New Way, is arising around Merezhkovsky. It is
half literary (in the new direction, of course) and
half religious, theological. This 'half' will be its un-
doing."[23]

It was not a fortunate alliance, for Merezhkovsky feared Briusov's Decadent influence on his new
journal,[24] while Briusov was dissatisfied because
Merezhkovsky was reluctant to publish Briusov's
poems in the journal. Briusov therefore questioned
seriously the advisability of entering into close relations with the journal.[25]

Whereas *Northern Flowers,* under the guidance
and sponsorship of "Skorpion," had served to unite
the St. Petersburg Symbolists with the Muscovites,
The New Way only brought into focus the basic
antagonism between the religious-philosophical program of the former and the esthetic program of

the latter. The Merezhkovskys' insistence that Briusov participate in their venture, despite the fact that
they were disdainful of Moscow Decadence in general
and feared Briusov in particular, further attests to
Briusov's growing prestige in Russian literary life.
According to D. Maksimov, the chief area of dispute
between Briusov on the one side and the Merezhkovskys and Pertsov on the other was not so much the
mystical, philosophic, and even reactionary nature of
the journal as it was the editors' attitude toward
artistic literature.[26]

   "The Moscow 'Decadents' with Briusov at their
head were primarily concerned with questions of
artistic craftsmanship and literary technique,"[27]
while these areas were of little or no concern to the
staff of *The New Way.* This disregard for literature
as such in favor of the new neo-Christian tendentiousness,[28] coupled with the Merezhkovskys' refusal to
print any substantial number of Briusov's poems
led to Briusov's final separation from the venture in
1903, the same year in which permission was granted
to publish *The Scales.*[29]

   During these years, which were devoted chiefly
to organizational and partisan activity, Briusov continued to make progress in his quest for recognition
as a poet in his own right. In 1903 "Skorpion" published his fourth collection of poems, *Urbi et Orbi,*
the title of which was meant to indicate that Briusov
was addressing himself not only to the "narrow city"
of his like-minded readers, but to the entire "world"
of Russian readers as well.[30] His like-minded readers
in the "narrow city" were, of course, duly impressed.
Blok wrote of Briusov's book that "its contents were
a series of unparalleled revelations, almost a work of
genius," and there is significant evidence that the
book played an important role in the future development of Blok's poetry.[31]

   But even more important for Briusov, the
"world" of the general reading public was more

responsive to *Urbi et Orbi* than to anything he had
previously written. The reviews of the work were,
of course, by no means unanimously favorable, and
the critics still called him "wild," and his verses
"perverse," but the reviewer for *The Russian Record*
(Russkie vedomosti) praised him for the "human"
element in his work, adding that "Briusov promises
further development in the future because he is
searching, and the sphere of his searchings is the
world of man."[32] Even more surprising was the review of Aleksandr Izmailov in *The New Illustrated*
(Novaia illiustratsiia), for Izmailov was a critic
known in Russian literary history for his hostility
toward Decadence and the "new ideas." After noting
that much of the book contains "typical" Decadent
verses, with a noticeable inclination toward mysticism, he remarks that the author undeniably possesses
"the poetic gift," "great literariness," and "poetic
mastery." Briusov's work is praised as both "tender"
and "deep."[33] Izmailov's review is of particular
interest, for he appears to be the first critic to recognize and remark upon the similarity of Briusov's
poetry to the poetry of Pushkin and his followers.
In retrospect this is not surprising if one considers
that since 1899 Briusov's interest in Russia's Golden
Age in general and in Pushkin in particular had been
steadily increasing. From 1899 through 1903 Briusov published eleven articles on Pushkin, Baratynsky, and Karolina Pavlovna, numerous book reviews,
and a book, *Letters from and to Pushkin: New
Materials Collected Under the Editorship of Valery
Briusov* (1903).

If Briusov's name was rapidly becoming well
known in Russian educated circles, it was not solely
due to his public activities in recruiting for the
movement, his work at "Skorpion," and his collections of verses. As early as 1903 the poet was becoming one of the most prolific writers of the Symbolist movement. From 1900 to 1903 alone his

bibliography contains at least ninety-five items. In addition to his articles in *Russian Archive* and *The New Way,* his collections, and his poems published in *Northern Flowers,* he was writing an annual review of Russian literature for the English periodical, *The Athenaeum* (a task he took over from Balmont in 1900), contributing several articles a year to *The Russian Leaflet (Russkii listok),* and producing a steady flow of articles on occultism for *Rebus.* But when in October, 1903, permission was granted to "Skorpion" to publish the "critical journal" *The Scales,* Briusov's literary activity for the next several years centered almost exclusively around this, his most successful creation.

Just how complete Briusov's involvement with *The Scales* really was can be seen in the following excerpt from his "Autobiography":

In 1904 the publishing house "Skorpion" founded its journal *The Scales,* and I, having quit *The New Way,* gave myself over to it entirely. During the course of four years I, together with S. A. Poliakov, edited *The Scales,* and I am able to say that during these years there was not one line in the journal which I had not examined as editor and had not read in proof. Moreover, an enormous number of articles, particularly of our beginning contributors, were most painstakingly reworked by me, and there were cases where it would have been more correct to place my name under an article signed by someone else.[34]

With the appearance of the introductory statement, "To Our Readers" and Briusov's lead article (or, better, manifesto), "The Keys of Mysteries," *(Kliuchi tain),* in the first issue of *The Scales* in January, 1904, Briusov had attained his goal: Russian Symbolism was no longer merely the creation of the journalists, and Briusov was the undisputed leader of Russian Symbolism.

CHAPTER FOUR

The Scales Years (1904-1905)

1. *The Scales* and the Shift from "Decadence" to "Symbolism" (1904-1905)

The years during which *The Scales* appeared
mark the zenith of Symbolism as a movement in
Russia. There will never be total agreement as to
whether the true nature of Russian Symbolism was
expressed by the "God-seeking" mysticism of St.
Petersburg or the estheticism of Moscow; but because the journal carried Briusov's unmistakable
stamp, *The Scales* did (in its first years, at least)
express the spirit of French Symbolism as it was ini-
tially conceived; and this was Briusov's understanding
of Symbolism as well. This is apparent in the journal's
interest in and representation of art and learning
in all its facets, in its distinctly international flavor,
in its devotion to poetry rather than to prose, and
in its concern with criticism and poetic theory even
more than with poetry itself:[1] "Nothing could be
more just than the definition of *The Scales* as the
'guardian of the indispensable principles of art' [the
phrase is Gippius']. The journal's greatest merit was
its fight against the stagnation of contemporary
Russian literary life" (Donchin, p. 66). As we shall
see below, the fight against this "stagnation" was
Briusov's major preoccupation until the Revolution.

The creation of the journal was no less important for Briusov's personal aspirations. With the pages
of the periodical and its editorial staff at his disposal,
Briusov became almost overnight the arbiter of
Russian literary taste. In his numerous theoretical
articles and critical reviews, he aimed at establishing
conclusively the hegemony of the "new art" in
Russia.

Although in its first year of publication, *The*

Scales was greeted with general hostility by all the non-Symbolist critics and reviews, by 1905 there was no doubt, either among Symbolism's adherents or its detractors, that the journal was the organ of Russia's dominant literary movement and that Briusov was its leader.[2] It is difficult to imagine the awe in which he was now held by his contemporaries. There was no longer anyone in the front ranks of Russian Modernism who was able to compete with Briusov. One point, however, should be made clear. Briusov's exalted position was by no means the result of mere politics and clever maneuvering. He was undoubtedly the most erudite man of letters of his time in Russia, and no less significantly—with the publication of *Urbi et Orbi*—one of its brightest poetic hopes. Briusov's erudition consisted of more than a highly specialized knowledge in one or two fields, as was the case with many of his contemporaries, for great as his passion for recognition and glory was, his maniacal quest for knowledge was even greater, and his thirst for knowledge, combined with his almost superhuman capacity for study and work, led to results which bordered on the phenomenal.

D. Maksimov has noted that whereas in the first years of their activity the Symbolists were engaged primarily in a battle with Naturalism and Realism their second struggle, after these forces were subdued, was chiefly one for the movement's "purity"; it was a struggle aimed at Symbolism's vulgarizers and epigones as well as at the pornographers and sensationalists who were attempting to share the limelight with the Symbolists.[3] *The Scales,* under the leadership of Briusov, was the leading organ in this struggle.

Formerly the only other figures on the Russian literary scene who might have laid claim to the title of leader were Merezhkovsky and Balmont. By the year 1904-1905, however, the brightest star in the

Valery Briusov

literary firmament was Briusov's. In a letter to his
father (March 8, 1904), Blok spoke of an "immea-
surably greater light" in Briusov than in the Merezhkovskys and expressed his belief that while Merezhkovsky had no more to say, Briusov "is greater
than all others."[4] As far as Balmont was concerned—
although as late as 1903 he was still at the "apogee
of his glory," and people were talking about the
"Balmontian epoch of Russian poetry"[5]—he had
now become outdated. By 1905 the nature of the
"new poetry" had undergone an essential change,
and Balmont belonged to the past. Briusov sensed
this change in Russian poetry, and he also sensed
what this meant for its former ruler: "[With Balmont's departure for Mexico] it is as though some
sort of period in our literature has ended. He ruled
freely for ten years in our poetry. But now the
warder has fallen from his hands. We have gone far
forward; he has remained in one place. Perhaps he
is a giant among us (as a poet, by his immediate
gift), but he is in the past... We are moving forward!"[6]
     Precisely what the nature of this change was
has already been alluded to above. The "new art"
was becoming mature, it was acquiring substance, a
genuine self-confidence in its own worth, and, gradually, even respectability. What had actually taken
place was the passing of Russian Modernism from
Decadence to Symbolism.
     Before elaborating on this new stage in the
history of Symbolism, we would do well to examine
the terms "Modernism," "Decadence," and "Symbolism" in greater detail. The term "modernism"
is a catchall to encompass the change in the direction
of Russian literature, which we have been calling
the "new ideas," away from Realism and Naturalism.
The term, then, will include all the literary movements in Russia subsequent to Realism and Naturalism and prior to Socialist Realism. Difficulties arise,
however, when we apply the terms "Decadence" and

[67]

"Symbolism." According to F. Reeve, the term
"decadence" was most frequently used in the following ways: "... first, like the French, as a label for the
'modernist' school; secondly, pejoratively by those
who for one reason or another were hostile to the
Symbolist movement; thirdly, by the Symbolists
themselves as a label for second-rate 'bohemian'
imitators; and fourthly, by the Symbolists again in
an ironic sense as a description of themselves."[7] Undoubtedly the term has been used in all of these
variations at one time or another. There is, however,
yet another sense. The term "Decadence" can be used
in a chronological and geographical sense, similar to
the sense of the division between the Moscow and
St. Petersburg "schools," with the Moscow group
the "Decadents" and the St. Petersburg group the
"Symbolists." This is particularly true of the early
period of Modernism.

James West in his study of Viacheslav Ivanov
and the Russian Symbolists writes: "It is customary
to divide the Russian Symbolists into an earlier,
'decadent' group, headed by Briusov and Balmont,
in which the influence of French and Belgian Symbolism is paramount, and a 'second generation,'
whose leading representatives were Ivanov, Bely,
and Blok, characterized by a more religious and
philosophical bent, less derivative, betraying in any
case the influence of German rather than French
sources, and not infrequently claiming to have roots
in a native Russian tradition. The turning point between the two is generally set at around 1904."[8]
This statement shows the chronological division
and stresses the "esthetic" versus the "philosophical"
division so characteristic of the Moscow-Petersburg
juxtaposition.

It appears that the Russian Symbolists themselves frequently used the terms in this sense. This
can be seen in the following passages from West's
book which attest to this usage of the term

Valery Briusov

"Decadence."

The decadent tendency—the religion of estheticism—gives a
different answer to this question: for the decadent, art is
divorced from life....
>   And just as *the distinguishing feature of Symbolism is
its realism,* (not on any account naturalism), *so decadence is
distinguished by its lack of realism, its illusionism, idealism,
and complete loss of the reality of the religious and mystical
experience.* (Modest Gofman, West, p. 118, my italics.)
>   *...False decadent individualism* supposes that the
assertion of individualism lies essentially in the affirmation
of separate, isolated random moments... (G. Chulkov, West,
p. 130, my italics.)

West himself writes:

Criticism of this kind was probably originally aroused by
the views expressed by certain of *the 'first-generation' Symbolists, the 'decadents';* for example, by Annensky's contention that 'poetic creations are in themselves incommen-
surate not only with the so-called real world, but even with
the logical, moral, and aesthetic aspects of the ideal world'.
More characteristic of *'second-generation' Symbolists* was
an attempt to claim for Symbolism some degree of realism....
(p. 148, my italics.)

These pronouncements also speak for a connection between the "chronological-geographical"
usage of the term "Decadence" and Reeve's "third
way," that is, "a label for second-rate 'bohemian'
imitators..." For these "bohemian" latecomers attempted to imitate the *early* Russian Symbolists,
that is the "Decadents," at least in dress and outrageous behaviors.
    These two usages legitimize the contention
that the word "Decadent" can be used conveniently
to signify the first stages of the Modernist movement,
for it was indeed in 1904-1905 that the so-called
"second-rate" 'bohemian' imitators" began to

appear. Consequently, we may call the period of
reaction against these imitators, the period beginning around 1905, the "Symbolist" period. These
distinctions will help to clarify the Symbolists' attacks against Decadence in the discussion below.

2. Briusov's Esthetic Views: "The New Realism" (1905)

By 1905 the complexion of Modernism's main-
stream, as noted above, had undergone a fundamental transition, one that might be characterized as a
transition from Decadence to Symbolism. Blok remarked on this fact in the same year: "Lately, and
for a long time already, there has been no trace of
[Decadence], and in my opinion in essence it does
not exist. It is taking shelter somewhere in Moscow,
among totally untalented "Grifians,' young gymnasium students who serve black masses (as though
in Berlin) and who, at meetings, talk boringly and
at length about black lilies. The real magicians, Briusov and others, who have essentially abandoned
Decadence long ago, gaze upon them with secret
gloom."[9]
Although Briusov had abandoned Decadence,
and here Blok is undoubtedly correct, it would be
fallacious to assume that he was now a Symbolist
in the same sense as Bely, Viacheslav Ivanov, Ellis,
and Blok himself, not to mention Merezhkovsky.
It was precisely the absence of any mystical philosophy or metaphysics to be served by the new art
that distinguished Briusov's brand of Symbolism
from that of the above-named poets. As Victor
Erlich points out, while Russian Symbolism—with
the very prominent exception of Briusov—sought
an "integrated world view... Verlaine, Laforgue,
and Mallarmé were primarily concerned with evol-
ving a new form of poetic expression."[10] For Briusov, and this is of particular importance, Symbolism

was rather Mallarméism (in Chulkov's expression),[11] that is, "a new form of poetic expression" should indeed be its only concern, whether in Russia or in Europe. Briusov would never have been able to agree with Viacheslav Ivanov's famous maxim that Russian Symbolism "could not be, and did not want to be merely art."[12] For Briusov there was no such thing as merely art, there was Art, and Art was not a metaphysic.

Certainly any consideration of Briusov's esthetic views must take into account which of his ideas were sincerely held and which were no more than "lip service" to the Symbolist "image." This is not an easy task; nevertheless, if we survey his critical and theoretical pronouncements over a longer period of time, say from 1895 to 1905, we are able to observe a decided degree of consistency in relation to certain views that would seem to have little bearing, if any, on the Symbolist "image" as such. We may, therefore, assume that these ideas and views are among those which were sincerely held by the poet and not maintained merely for propagandizing purposes.

Perhaps the fundamental difference between Briusov's estimation of Symbolism's place in art and that of his many opponents is to be found in his basic conception of art. In his opinion no literary school was an end unto itself, but only a way station along the road of art's eternal evolution. This view was made evident as early as 1897 when Briusov delivered an address entitled "Toward a History of Symbolism." In it he stated, "...individual literary schools—and among them Symbolism as well—are only stages, moments in this evolution [of modern poetry]."[13] He sees Symbolism as continuing the work begun by the Romantics and furthered by the pre-Raphaelites who "judged and rejected the form and content of previous poetry" and "cleared the way for the new poetry" (p. 271). Now these

movements have yielded to Symbolism, the mission
of which "is to create a new poetical language, to
rework the means of poetry anew" (p. 272). For
Briusov, poetry and art seem to be developing according to a natural progression, the eventual goal
of which is "freedom in art." Symbolism is only a
tool to be used in attaining this freedom; thus he
writes in "Toward a History of Symbolism": "I do
not hope that Symbolism will develop further. It is
only a transitionary stage [on the road] to the new
poetry. Apparently it has already fulfilled its task.
The old poetry is lying in ruins... At the same time,
Symbolism has created a totally new organ (not yet
put to the test) for the transmission of the soul's
innermost dynamics" (p. 274).

The above remarks, to be sure, did not reflect
Briusov's final views; they do, however, reflect his
esthetic point of departure as far as Symbolism is
concerned and this never changed.

We can see the continuity of his thought in
the next statement of his artistic beliefs (and his
first protracted one), *On Art,* which appeared in
1899.[14] This work contains many thoughts previously voiced by the poet, chiefly in his letters to
P. P. Pertsov, in the introductions to his various
publications, and in "Toward a History of Symbolism."

In *On Art* Briusov maintains that art serves to
"preserve for all time" the moment that has passed.[15]
It is the only means by which human experience
may be preserved; but he who is able to recognize
the fleeting moment as such, that is, as an important, never-to-be-repeated part of existence, also
possesses the two most important traits of the true
creator: the ability to recognize himself, his own
soul, and the even more essential ability *to understand* his soul. What sets the artist apart from the
others who may possess these abilities of self-recog-
nition and self-understanding is his capacity to retell

[72]

Valery Briusov

what he has understood in a manner that will make
it accessible to the souls of other individuals (p. 13).

We may here observe what—to Briusov's way
of thinking—can be considered the only true justification of art; art is justified because it is an act of
communication. The soul is ordinarily isolated because each man's perception of the world about
him is unique. From an awareness of this isolation
comes the need to communicate one's vision to the
souls of other men, and, ideally, to find a unity
with them. According to Briusov such a unity of
souls is possible only through art (p. 22),[16] however,
never through "art for art's sake" (p. 14).

Briusov makes an important distinction here.
Usually we tend to juxtapose the concept of art for
art's sake to that of "utilitarian art." Invariably
when in the context of Russian literary history we
think of "utilitarian art" we associate it with the
credos of the men of the sixties and seventies; on
the other hand, the concept of "art for art's sake"
is more often than not associated with the names
of the early Symbolists, particularly Balmont and
Annensky. But Briusov, generally considered a
"pure esthete," declares that "there is no sense
in art for art's sake" (p. 14). Real art—"utilitarian
art" in the Briusovian sense—contains but one characteristic, originality; "art always creates something
new" (p. 14).[17] And originality comes only at the
time of inspiration, that is, during "a moment of
greater feeling" (p. 14).

It is important to note, however, that this
"inspired originality" is not necessarily an originality
of content. Purely innovative *form* has its own
value. While defending Balmont's genius in a letter
to Pertsov, Briusov simultaneously defends the integrity of the value of poetry in and for itself. Pertsov had attacked Balmont for the latter's deviations
from reality. Briusov replied: "And don't you consider it worth anything that this deviation from

[73]

reality makes it possible for Balmont to introduce unheard of words into his poetry, to become intoxicated by the exotic names? ...Can it be true that you do not know how to enjoy verse as verse—exclusive of its content—only its sound, only its images, only its rhymes?"[18]

In the same letter Briusov explicitly details his belief that the act of poetic communication is not attained solely through content, that is, through ideas expressed by words alone; there is no way of knowing if the ideas expressed by a lyricist are really his own sincerely held precepts or whether they came upon him while in an "alien mood." Better to become united with the poet's thoughts through his art than through the ideas expressed in his semantics, for "...in every verse, in the deployment of words, in the selection of epithets, everywhere the poet remains himself, preserves his individuality and, consequently, his world view, his philosophy. How can one find it there? How can one gather gleams in a wisp of light?"[19]

The contention that Briusov was a "pure esthete," an adherent of "art for art's sake" is difficult to defend. The "art for art's sake" proponent is interested only in the communication of beauty, if he is interested in any communication at all. On the other hand, whereas Briusov is vitally concerned with communicating the message contained in the artist's "soul," he denies that the artist, and specifically the Symbolist, has any special universal, transcendental truth to communicate.

The above directs our attention to a further fundamental difference between Briusov's esthetic ideas and those of the St. Petersburg Symbolists— Merezhkovsky and Viacheslav Ivanov—as well as others of the so-called "later generation"; this difference lies in Briusov's attitudes toward craftsmanship and toward the concept of "the literary school." In *On Art* he writes concerning the craft:

Valery Briusov

"It is imperative to be acquainted with the external devices of an artistic creation, imperative to make oneself completely familiar with them. For in art there is much that is conventional and which will long continue to be conventional. *Mood* [that is, content] *and that in which it is expressed—words, sounds, and tints—are heterogeneous*" (p. 18, my italics).

With this passage in mind, we are better able to understand Briusov's devotion to technical mastery. We are also better able to understand why his intense study of the technical aspects of poetry was greeted with such contempt by many of his critics. Briusov's critics, chiefly other poets, were not aware that their conception of the nature of inspiration and Briusov's were fundamentally different. Content and form were "heterogeneous" for Briusov, for the others "homogeneous." Briusov finds the total work of art derived from three sources: 1) inspiration and resultant content come from within the artist himself, 2) images and coloring come from the epoch, and, 3) technique comes from the literary school (p. 19).[20]

According to Briusov, "a school of art only teaches external devices" (p. 18), and consequently "the works of the same school coincide with each other according to [these external, creative] devices" (p. 22). But even though these works may be similar as far as devices, they may be, and more often than not are, "totally different one from another in terms of content" (p. 22).

Thus the dichotomy between Briusov's brand of Symbolism and Symbolism as understood by the "God-seeking," "mystical," or "theurgical" poets becomes clear. As stated previously, art was never "merely art" for Briusov, and at the same time it was never the handmaiden of metaphysics. Similarly, Briusov felt that Symbolism, too, *as a school* never played the role of Bearer of the Word.

He saw Symbolism's contribution to art primarily as twofold: first, it continued the battle begun by Romanticism against artistic inhibition (p. 23), and second, it had "correctly evaluated the meaning of words for the artist" (p. 24). And it is in this belief in the role of words that Bruisov was a Symbolist, a Symbolist in the French sense, in the sense of impressions, moods, hints, and correspondences, in the sense of a continuation of Romanticism.

But Briusov's fellow Russian Symbolists, too, shared this respect for the power of words and their role in art. Their divergent path is to be found in their attitude toward the movement. For the others Symbolism was the one true faith, the faith without which art was unattainable. For Briusov, who was ready "to worship Christ and Satan," the essence of an artistic work was not to be found in the doctrine or metaphysics of the artist's school, rather, "the essence of an artistic work is the soul of its creator, *and it is all the same by what means one approaches it"* (p. 25, my italics).

Although Briusov was more than once to modify his esthetic theory, he never deviated in his attitude toward literary schools and their role. And in the end result it was precisely this attitude, which elevated the individual's pathos over that of the school, that was at the root of his subsequent split with the movement. Although Briusov eventually stopped preaching the doctrine of "extreme individualism" which characterized his earliest days, he never stopped believing in it and creating and working in accordance with it.

The poet's attitude toward literary schools, and toward Symbolism in particular, was a wary one at best even as early as 1895 when he expressed his dismay that Symbolism was being misunderstood as a movement, as a school:

Poor Symbolism! What isn't ascribed to it; it seems there is no term more indefinite. . . . There is a whole group of critics

Valery Briusov

who . . . maintain that Symbolism is the rebirth of ideological poetry [*ideinoi poezii*] , or better, the rebirth of the idea
in poetry. In my opinion Symbolism and the rebirth of ideological content [*ideinosti*] are two totally separate currents
in the new poetry; currents that can merge but that can also
exist separately, and indeed, more often than not they do
exist separately.[21]

Thus, as early as 1899 with the appearance of
On Art Briusov's initial esthetic views were already
formulated firmly, and formulated in such a manner
as to place him from the outset in a position diametrically opposed to that of the other leading figures
of Russian Symbolism.

In general, Briusov's activities during the 1900's
show that advance in the level of contemporary art
was his primary aim in literature. His most pressing
concerns in this period have been summarized as
follows by N. S. Gornitskaia: " . . . the role and
significance of literature, the relationship of literature to life, the writer's creative laboratory, the paths
of literature's development, the evaluation of literary movements and the work of individual writers,
Russian as well as West European, and the particulars
of poetic craftsmanship."[22] What is most significant
in this summation is the obvious fact that Briusov's
literary occupations become increasingly less parochial; Symbolism as such, as a localized, specific,
literary school, is superseded by the greater consideration of the future of literature in general.

Briusov was not concerned merely with destroy-
ing the imitators and vulgarizers of Symbolism. For
him it was of much greater importance to make the
truly first-class artists aware of the real nature and
progressive role of Symbolism in the ever-advancing
process of literary development. As noted above,
Symbolism had already become only nominally important to Briusov as a literary *school.* The movement was of concern in that it expressed, in his
opinion, the highest level of poetic artistry yet

attained by man. As one follows Briusov's subsequent
enterprises, and as one observes his relations with his
fellow Symbolists becoming gradually more and more
strained, one comes to understand that in the years
1905 to 1909 his life's work revolved around a ten-
sion between the beginning of the apparent stagnation of Symbolism and his truly herculean efforts to
lead the movement onward to the next evolutionary
level of art, what we shall call in what follows "the
new Realism" in poetics.

 Although Briusov's best work, *Stephanos* (1906),
was yet to come, from the time he began his activities
with *The Scales* in 1904 until his death in 1924, he
was most important in the history of Russian literature as a missionary and teacher of poetic skill and
artistic integrity.[23]

 In January, 1905, Briusov published in *The Scales*
an article "The Sacred Sacrifice" ("Sviashchennaia
zhertva"). The article shows the new trends in Briusov's esthetic thought. In retrospect it is of particular
interest since it may be considered the real beginning
of his break with Symbolism as it was then known. He
addresses himself here chiefly to the relation of art
to life and to the question of realism in art. [24]

 Although Briusov still clings to the rather mysti-
cal-sounding phrases that were so characteristic of his
earlier writings and that resounded so strongly in his
manifesto "Keys to the Mysteries" in the in-
naugural issue of *The Scales,* in "The Sacred
Sacrifice" his essentially non-mystical, non-philosophical orientation toward poetry begins to assert
itself perceptibly. In spite of the "unextinguishable
altar fires," the "fire of the Vestal'" and "the sacri-
ficial knives,"[25] Briusov states his belief quite explicitly that art must not be divorced from life, that
art must preserve within itself the artist's world
view, not as created specifically for a poetic work,
but as an expression of his experience. In the past
it had always seemed quite natural for the poet to

Valery Briusov

hold one view of life in his verses and another in
"real life" (p. 24). Whereas in the Pushkinian period
of Russian poetry only a very few poets were able
to bring their true feelings, emotions, and beliefs
into their poetry, "the abyss between the artist's
'words' and 'deeds' disappeared for us when it
turned out that *a creation is merely the reflection
of life, and nothing more"* (p. 27, my italics).

Briusov then states what we may regard as his
artistic creed. Although the images he employs are
calculated to appeal to the most mystical of Symbolists, we sense in his message his complete devotion
to art and his fanatical dedication to both artistic
integrity and the total merging of the artist's life
with his work: "We demand from the poet that he
unwearyingly make his 'sacred sacrifices' not only
with his poetry, but with every hour of his life, with
his every feeling, with his love, his hate, his achievements, and his failures. Let him create not his books,
but his life. Let him keep the altar flame unexting-
uished, as the fire of the Vestal, let him be enveloped
by the great pyre, fearing not that it consume his life.
On the altar of our society we cast ourselves. Only
the sacrifical knife cleaving the breast gives one the
right to the name of poet" (p. 29). When we consider
that this passage in the article's context is a refutation
of Pushkin's attitude to the poet's role as expressed in
his lines from "The Poet,"

> Until Apollo summons
> The poet for a sacred sacrifice,
> He is cravenly submerged
> In the vain world's cares;
> His holy lyre is silent;
> His soul partakes of fervid sleep,
> And among the world's insignificant children,
> He, perhaps, is more insignificant than all.[26]

we immediately think of the sharply contrasting lines
in Briusov's own poem, "To the Poet": "Perhaps

[79]

everything in life is but a means/for brightly singing verses."[27]

As Victor Erlich reminds us, "these lines were quoted *ad nauseam* in the pre-1914 Russian literary *cénacles.*"[28] When Erlich deduces from these lines, however, "Briusov's programmatic repudiation of a strong emotional involvement" (p. 78), he seems to be sharing with the poet's earlier critics their condemnation of Briusov's "cold-blooded" attitude toward life, and the subsequent reflection of this attitude in the emotional sterility of Briusov's verse. Evidently criticism has neglected to consider the true intensity and significance of Briusov's artistic dedication. To quote Erlich again, he sees these lines as the poetic expression of "the notion that the poet has the right, indeed the duty, to use his life as material for his work, and to hoard momentary thrills in order to produce more and better love lyrics. . . ." (p. 77).

This contention is doubtlessly true for many poets of the period (and, especially, of the Romantic period which Erlich also treats in his book), and indeed often for Briusov himself. That Briusov was frequently an opportunist in the most negative sense of the word in his relations with others has been irrefutably and gleefully documented by Khodasevich and Tsvetaeva, among others. But we do Briusov an injustice if we evaluate the poet's sincerity on the basis of these lines alone. Briusov is not merely seeking a means "to produce more and better love lyrics," but is attempting, as he explicitly states in "The Sacred Sacrifice," to make poetry a way of life, to prevent poetry from being divorced from life and life from poetry. That such a vision may be "unrealistic" or "romantic" is irrelevant; the objective is admirable; for the goal of such a vision is absolute artistic sincerity and integrity. Briusov suspects, and most likely correctly, that to set aside a period of time for the creation of poetry is an unnatural division

of poetry from life and must result in artificial
emotions finding their expression in the artist's creation. Certainly long before Briusov's exhortation,
poets were using life's experiences at the time of their
consummation as a "means for brightly singing
verses." In the same poem Briusov commands: "At
moments of love's embraces/Force yourself to be
dispassionate." Is this not what Goethe describes in
the *Römische Elegien* when he writes:

>   Uberfällt sie der Schlaf, lieg ich und denke mir
> viel. Oftmals hab ich auch schon in ihren Armen gedichtet
>   Und des Hexameters Mass leise mit fingernder Hand
> Ihr auf den Rücken gezählt.[29]

It is customary to see Briusov's callousness,
which resulted in the "insincere," "shallow" features
of his verses, in what Erlich calls in *The Double Image*
"the curious impersonality" of Briusov's poetry,
where his verses' "sensuality is more convincing
than their emotionality" (p. 78). This critical attitude ignores the poet's own esthetic criteria. Just as
Briusov is criticized for his addiction to craftsmanship in place of so-called divine inspiration, so, too
is he taken to task for his impersonality instead of
emotionality.

One is struck by the thought that had Briusov
been writing in England at the time instead of Russia, he might today share a place in modern poetry's
pantheon with Ezra Pound and T. S. Eliot, the
latter so closely associated with the "impersonal
theory of poetry," a theory that emphasizes craftsmanship and minimizes "emotionality."

If one equates "sensuality" (Erlich) with "feeling" and then juxtaposes "feeling" to "emotion,"
one sees that Briusov's poetry , in this respect at
least, conforms perfectly to criteria laid down by
Eliot in one of his most famous essays, "Tradition
and the Individual Talent"; for example: "The

business of the poet is not to find new emotions, but to use the ordinary ones and, in working them up into poetry, to express feelings which are not in actual emotions at all. And emotions which he has never experienced will serve his turn as well as those familiar to him."[30] We shall see below that such a stance is an essential part of Briusov's mature esthetic.

It is the present author's opinion that the typical Briusovian lack of emotionality is not demonstrative of inspirational poverty or insincerity, but is the poetic reflection of an esthetic attitude (perhaps incipient in Briusov since his earliest days) that began to emerge as an explicit philosophy in 1905 with the publication of his article "The Sacred Sacrifice."

In this light it is interesting and informative to dwell upon the curious parallels between Briusov's developing esthetic and the respective attitudes toward poetry and the poet subsequently championed by Ezra Pound, T. S. Eliot, and Paul Valéry, particularly in relation to questions of craftsmanship, emotion, and inspiration (in the Romantic sense).

Pound, Eliot, and Valéry, whose names, too, are associated with the "new ideas" in their countries, may be classified as Symbolists, as Edmund Wilson does in his book, *Axel's Castle*.[31] If they are Symbolists, and certainly those may be found who would deny this, they are "new" Symbolists in that they were breaking with contemporary poetic custom and bringing forth a new dimension in poetry, a dimension of coolness, scholarship, craftsmanship, and impersonality. This was naturally more of an innovation in the cases of Pound and Eliot than it was with Valéry who had his country's traditional preoccupation with poetic craftsmanship behind him in both the Parnassian and Symbolist schools.

In general, one may say that Symbolism in the persons of the four poets under discussion was now losing its neo-Romantic aspect and adopting certain criteria favored by Realism. Since the term neo-Realism is already an established one, we will call this new development in Symbolist poetry "the new Realism."

Essentially what Briusov was after, beginning with his ideas as expressed in "The Sacred Sacrifice," was a poetry as technically perfect as the best work of the Parnassians and free from the "God-seeking" mysticism of the works of the Russian Symbolists. On the other hand, the absence of mysticism does not condone the absence of content or affirm "art for art's sake" (see above). Rather, Briusov was proposing that poetry be intimately related to the poet's life and to reality in general and that sincerity in creation was the prime prerequisite for attaining to such an aim (hence his repudiation of Pushkin's poem "The Poet").

The point of departure for this entire approach is the question of inspiration. In general inspiration or, better, its source and nature was of considerable significance to Pound, Eliot, and Valéry as well as to Briusov, and in their pronouncements on the subject we can observe the emerging concept of "the artist as scientist."

Pushkin was perhaps the first Russian literary figure to make the connection between science and art when he wrote that "inspiration is necessary in geometry as well as in poetry." Significantly, Briusov quotes this line in "The Sacred Sacrifice" (p. 25). These words seem to be an echo of Valéry's when in 1889 he wrote that the poet "is no longer the disheveled madman who writes a whole poem in the course of one feverish night, he is a cool scientist, almost an algebraist, in the service of a subtle dreamer.... Everything the poet has imagined, felt, dreamed, and planned will be passed through a sieve, weighed, filtered, subjected to form, and condensed as much as possible...."[32] Eliot, in an

introduction to Valéry's book, views the poet's observations as sound advice:

The insistence in Valéry's poetics upon the small part played
in the elaboration of a poem by what he calls *le rêve*—what
is ordinarily called the "inspiration"—and upon the subsequent process of deliberate, conscious, ardous labor, is a
most wholesome reminder to the young poet. It is corrective
of that romantic attitude which, in employing the word
"inspiration," inclines consciously or unconsciously to
regard the poet's role in the composition of a poem as
mediumistic and irresponsible (p. xii).

And finally, Ezra Pound, Eliot's earliest cham-
pion and his mentor in many areas, most particularly in poetic craftsmanship, was inordinately fond of
likening art to science. For example, in *The Spirit
of Romance* he writes: "Poetry is a sort of inspired
mathematics, which gives us equations, not for
abstract figures, triangles, spheres, and the like, but
equations for human emotions."[33] In an article
quoted by his biographer and published in *The New
Freewoman* in 1913 entitled "The Serious Artist,"
Pound asserts that the arts are a science "just as
chemistry is," and that they "give us a great per-
centage of the lasting unassailable data regarding the
nature of man, of immaterial man, of man considered as a thinking and sentient creature" (p. 141).
Pound continues his analogy by comparing the
consequences of insincerity and artificiality in both
art and science by maintaining that "an artist who
'falsifies his report' for whatever reason, is no better
than a doctor or scientist who falsifies his, and
should be punished or despised in proportion to the
seriousness of his offense" (p. 142).

Hence we see that the foundation of what we
have called "the new Realism" in poetics is based
upon two essential suppositions: that the artist
approach his calling with what we might understand as a "realistic" or "scientific" sincerity, and

Valery Briusov

that the stuff of poetry be life, real life, the artist's life. On the other hand, this intimate relation between the artist's life and his poetry must not be expressed in romantic emotionality; rather the subjective element indispensable to such poetry must be subordinate to the criteria of the poetic craft. As Briusov pointedly instructed Bely in his polemical article, "In Defense from Certain Praise" ("V zashchitu ot odnoi pokhvaly"), "poets may be measured by the worth and shortcomings of their poetry and not by anything else...." especially not by whether "the Apocalypse" tells in their work or by "how they relate to 'The Woman Enveloped in Sun'. "[34] In this same article, Briusov stresses once again the necessity for criticizing poetry on the basis of its intrinsic merit and warns against the consequences of a biased approach to poetry. He cautions Bely: "The critics of the 60's evaluated poets according to their relation to the progressive ideas of their time. They discarded Fet from their scheme, you Balmont." (p. 38).

These remarks addressed to Bely show how, at a very early point in the movement's history (1905), Briusov's non-mystical, non-philosophical orientation toward poetry began to come between him and the movement he had created. In his study of Briusov, Kornei Chukovsky notes the important fact that "in the Decadent's camp, Briusov was the only person without a [mystical or metaphysical] philosophy," and it was precisely this fact that enabled him to reply polemically to the mystical experiences of Bely and Viacheslav Ivanov with his "common-sense syllogisms."[35]

One cannot overemphasize the importance of "The Sacred Sacrifice" as an indicator of what was to become the foundation of Briusov's esthetic position for the remainder of his life. It is in this article that he expounds most fully his ideas on "Symbolism as Realism" and explains his thoughts in an historical context. It will be worthwhile to examine these ideas in more detail.

Briusov calls his readers' attention to the fact that the earliest representatives of Symbolism— Baudelaire for example—made their appearance during the height of literary Realism and that the new Symbolists "would have been impossible without Balzac...."[36] By the same token, the Symbolists came from the ranks of the Parnassians and took from them "only an understanding of form and of its significance," while leaving them "to collect their trophies" (p. 26). Thus, with an understanding of life garnered from the Realists and an appreciation of form and artistic craftsmanship taken from the Parnassians, the Decadents turned their eyes and inspiration to the "fires and the hammers of the factories, to the thunder of trains... to the common furnishings of contemporary rooms... to all the tortuous contradictions of the modern soul... to that contemporaneity that the Realists hoped to embody" (p. 26). Briusov finishes this section of his article with what he must have understood as a firm statement of his belief that the history and development of poetry is an organic whole: "It is not coincidental that the City of our days, which first entered art in the Realistic novel, found its best bards precisely within the ranks of the Decadents.... The new Symbolist creation was the natural consequence of the Realist school; it was the new, further, inescapable step in the development of art" (pp. 26-27).

One should not understand by the foregoing that Briusov was making a case for modern poetry's being no more than the Realistic novel in poetic form, similar to the verse of Nekrasov. The fundamental difference between Realism and Symbolism is that after the Symbolists learned that life is the only subject for art, they turned their search inward, while the Realists sought it from without (p. 27); for

the Symbolists had taken the Realists' truth a step
further with the realization that "the entire world
is within me." (p. 26). With this new knowledge
came the artist's new task, "to express his experiences which are the only reality accessible to our
consciousness...." (p. 27).

After inspiration the next fundamental aspect
of "the new Realism" in poetics is the question of
craftsmanship, which question also involves the juxtaposition of "possessed" poet versus the "maker"
(in Wellek's and Warren's expression).[37] Briusov's
concern with form and craft has been mentioned
often enough to allow one to realize that it was a
lasting preoccupation with the poet from his
earliest days. How enduring it became is readily
apparent when one recalls some of the titles of his
later period: *Experiments in Metrics and Rhythm
System, Euphony and Assonances, Strophic System
and Forms (Opyty po metrike i ritmike, po evfonii i
sozvuchiiam, po strofike i formam [1918]), The
Science of Verse (Nauka o stikhe [1919]), Funda-
mentals of the Study of Prosody (Osnovy stikho-
vedeniia [1924]),* and *Problems of Poetics (Prob-
lemy poetiki [1925]).*

Once again the similarities between Briusov's
appreciation of and insistence on poetic craftsmanship and that of Pound, Eliot, and Valéry is striking.
Valéry's position on this question and Eliot's may
be demonstrated by the words of the latter in regard to the former:

A corollary, perhaps, of Valéry's emphasis upon fundamental
"brainwork" (is not the phrase Dante Rossetti's?) is his insistence upon the value for the poet of the exercise of difficult and complicated rhyming stanza forms. No poet was
ever more conscious of the benefit of working in strict forms,
the advantage to be gained by imposing upon oneself limitations to overcome. Such exercises... can teach the genuine
poet... the way in which form and content must come to
terms. It is only by practicing the sonnet, the sestina, or the

villanelle that we learn what sort of content can *not* be expressed in each of these forms.[38]

Given Briusov's life-long devotion to form and craft, it is not surprising that he quoted the following lines of Théophile Gautier on the poet as a worker in "The Sacred Sacrifice": "A poet... is above all a worker. The endeavor to place him on an ideal pedestal is totally senseless. He must have exactly as much sense as any worker and is obligated to know his job" (p. 25). The idea of poet as worker immediately calls to mind the well-known poem in which Briusov compares his dream with a faithful ox. Of course his critics have derided him endlessly for these lines; however, they provide insight into Briusov's ceaseless praise of hard labor.

> Forward my dream, my faithful ox!
> By force if not by choice.
> I am close, my knout is heavy,
> I myself am laboring, and you, work![39]

It is perhaps Ezra Pound, however, who in his erudition and endless study, as well as in many other details of his life in art, is most similar to Briusov as far as his attitude toward craft is concerned. Pound's biographer, Noel Stock, tells us that Pound believed "the 'Impulse,' as he called it, was from the gods, but that technique was a man's own responsibility; and so he resolved that at thirty he would know more about poetry than any man living."[40]

Briusov's career included a constant struggle against the "Romantic" tradition of prophetic inspiration at the expense of hard work and study. He found it inexplicable, for example, that musicians and artists spent the greater part of their lives practicing and studying, first as students and then even at the height of their fame, whereas the poet who studied and practiced the forms of poetry as exercise was considered an uninspired clod.[41] The same

Valery Briusov

held true for painters and sculptors, artists who
spent years and years as students before even thinking of setting out on their own. This, however, is
not to say that Briusov felt that anyone could be
a poet; just as Pound felt that only the "impulse"
came from the gods, so too did Briusov maintain
that "it is impossible to learn to be an artist; this is
a born gift; but it is impossible to be an accomplished
artist without study.... Hardly anyone thinks of the
fact that the poet is a teacher of mankind. and that
a teacher is supposed to know more than his pupils"
(The Far and the Near, p. 118).

By the beginning of 1906, Briusov had reached
his esthetic maturity and had overcome the narrow
bias of parochial artistic interests. Symbolism as a
school had served its purpose, both for Briusov, by
propelling him to the front ranks of Russia's literary
luminaries, and for the advance of Russian literature
in general, by finally freeing it from the tight stric-
tures of the second half of the nineteenth century.

The biggest problem now facing Briusov was
how to survive as a non-partisan littérateur in a
literary society dominated by partisan adherents of
various schools and philosophies, each vying with
the other for recognition as literature's "true faith."
As a result, the remaining years of Briusov's association with the movement proved to be a chronicle
of the intense competitions raging in Russian literary
circles at that time, a chronicle of genius and mediocrity, loyalty and betrayal, pathetic stagnation and
brilliant advance.

CHAPTER FIVE

The Scales Years and After (1906-1924)

1. The Decline of Decadence (1906-1907)

In the beginning of 1906 "Skorpion" published Briusov's fifth collection of poetry, *Venok* (or *Stephanos;* this title appeared in Greek on the book's binding). The appearance of this book is significant for several reasons. It was Briusov's "first relatively major success."[1] Moreover, it showed conclusively that in terms of poetic talent Briusov was more akin to the nineteenth century than the twentieth.[2] Briusov himself was intensely aware of this fact, as is evident from a letter written in January, 1907, to E. A. Liatsky: "...although from the outside I seem to be the leader of those whom... we call our Decadents, in reality among them I am like a hostage in the enemy's camp. For a long time everything that I have been writing and everything that I say is decidedly not in the spirit of my literary comrades, and I must admit that I do not like what they are writing and saying."[3] As a result of the success of *Stephanos,* Briusov began to receive invitations to publish in the "fat journals," until now closed both to him and to the majority of the other Symbolist poets.[4] Soon he was publishing his work in *God's World (Mir Bozhii)* and *Education (Obrazovanie).*[5] Finally, Briusov now at last achieved his poetic maturity. The poetry in *Stephanos* was different from anything he had written before. As D. S. Mirsky points out, the cycle "The Eternal Truth of Idols" ("Pravda vechnaia kumirov") "was the center and zenith of Briusov's creation; [it] is one of the best adornments of our new poetry. In it [Briusov] attained style and total adequateness of form, that is, the highest an artist may attain."[6]

The fact that what we now understand to be

Briusov's mature style—though this style was to be
changed again later on—had little in common with
the style of most of the other young writers of the
period shows how the gap that existed between
him and his collaborators at *The Scales* was widening.
And this gap became even greater when Briusov
came into closer contact with the editorial staffs of
the "fat journals" who were, by and large, much
more conservative in their literary tastes than those
people grouped around *The Scales* and the other
Modernist publishing houses and journals. The reason
that this more conservative side of Russian literary
criticism praised *Stephanos* even before Briusov's
own allies did so, was precisely because the poet's
inherent poetic conservatism is so evident in the
work. The book displays what Mirsky calls a "lofti-
ness," and is the victory of "high poetry" (p. 418)
over the diet of innovative, radical, more often than
not second-rate poetry that was flooding the reading
public now that Modernism had gained such wide
favor. Even when Modernist poetry was not at all
second rate, as in the case of Bely, Blok, Merezhkovsky, Z. Gippius, and Viacheslav Ivanov, it was very
seldom to the public's taste.

Briusov was hardly sorry for the increased dis-
tance between him and the other Symbolists. It is
safe to assume that Briusov, whose poetical talents
and interests were so far ranging, felt constricted by
his self-imposed identification with a particular
literary school. As Chulkov correctly notes, "Briusov
was really afraid of Symbolism, for he felt that
Symbolism obligated, and he wanted to remain un-
attached whatever the world view might be. As early
as *Tertia Vigilia* he declared 'that there are as many
truths in the world as there are thoughts and
words'."[7] Even in 1905 Briusov had complained of
the confining limits of Decadence to V. S. Miroliubov, the publisher of *The Journal for All (Zhurnal
dlia vsekh)*: "Collaboration with *The Journal for*

Valery Briusov

All is dear to me to the highest degree because it is
the only way in which my poems can break out of
the narrow circle of admirers of Decadent poetry."[8]
Most likely it was not merely the fact that Decadence imposed confining demands that caused this
confession, but rather Briusov's dissatisfaction with
what was taking place in its name. It seems that even
at this early date (the summer of 1905) Briusov
thought he was through with *The Scales,* although,
as it turned out, this was not the case. The day after
he wrote the above letter to Miroliubov, he wrote
Georgy Chulkov that "I have definitely quit my
editorship and will only remain a ... contributor."[9]

Of course "Decadence" as it had been known
in Russia up to this time was a thing of the past, even
at "Skorpion." Briusov was cognizant of this, as
were Andrei Bely, Aleksandr Blok, Viacheslav Ivanov,
and Georgy Chulkov, the leading "ideological"
spokesman for Modernism. Blok made this quite
clear in a review of *Stephanos* that appeared in 1906:
"The notion of 'Decadence' in the narrow sense has
passed into the history of literature. By now it either
means nothing or is a disparaging word."[10] A problem arises, however, in understanding "Decadence"
in the "broad sense." For it is in the new lines that
were being drawn between the various factions of
the Symbolist school that the seeds of the later,
final disruption of Decadence are to be found. In
general 1906 marks yet another turning point in the
history of Russian Symbolism. As noted by V. Orlov, in this year Symbolism, a unified school, tightly
and cohesively grouped around *The Scales* and
"Skorpion" in Moscow, changed from a school per
se into a disparate conglomerate of "movements."[11]
Decadence thus had not only passed from the literary scene, but the term Symbolism, beginning in 1906,
became so ambiguous as to be totally meaningless as
a concept. The range of factions seemed to grow
without end..There were mystics, adherents of

eschatology and anarchy, neo-Populists, and neo-
Kantians.[12] The split of the "school" into movements is also attested to by the sudden proliferation
of new publishing houses, journals, and almanacs.
In Moscow 1906 saw the founding of *The Golden
Fleece (Zolotoe runo)* and *The Divide (Pereval).* In
St. Petersburg the publishing house "Ory" became
the center of activity for Viacheslav Ivanov and
Blok, while Chulkov's almanac *Torches (Fakely)*
also had its presses in the same city and worked
closely with "Ory."

While the various factions all had their own
axes to grind and causes to espouse, it was Viacheslav Ivanov, Aleksandr Blok, and Georgy Chulkov
who became the chief challengers to *The Scale's*
hegemony over Symbolist esthetic philosophy, which
is the same as saying that they became Briusov's (and,
until 1910, Bely's) mortal ideological enemies.

The fact that both the Scalesites and the members of Ivanov's rival movement (for he was the undisputed leader of the dissident group) carried on
their polemics from 1906 until 1910 under the
banner of Symbolism should not obscure the fact
that the struggle actually concerned the purpose
of art. Thus, when Briusov and Bely on the one
hand and Ivanov and Blok on the other speak about
"Symbolism," the reader is well advised to understand "art" in its place. This protracted argument
essentially revolved around the question: is art truly
art in the sense of the expression of personal feelings
and emotions, distinguished from the non-artistic
by the elements of form and beauty, or does it serve
the purpose of creating religious myths and pro-
viding a collective religious experience? The partisans
of *The Scales* adhered to the former proposition
while Ivanov, Blok, and their followers adhered to
the latter.

Implicit in the above antinomy is, of course,
the question of "extreme individualism" (the first

[93]

Valery Briusov

and most enduring tenet of the Decadents) versus
the "overcoming of individualism" (the aim of Ivanov's group). Stated in yet another way, the controversy can be seen as "personal freedom in art" versus "metaphysical freedom." The latter, according
to Ivanov, is what occurs when artistic creation is
"elevated to the theurgic will" and one arrives at
the "metaphysical boundaries," that is, at the "super-
personal" *(sverkhlichnoe)*.[13]

Ivanov and his followers believed that mankind was about to transcend the limitations of
"differentiation" and individualism.[14] Symbolism
would provide the means for accomplishing this
task. Earlier Ivanov had identified the Greek God
Dionysus with Christ. Consequently, the essence of
Symbolism (that is, "art"), the purpose of which
was to serve Christ, would be Dionysian.[15] With
such an understanding of the nature of art (or Symbolism), Apollonian art, that is, the esthetically
oriented art of the "Decadents," becomes Ivanov's
direct antagonist. For Ivanov the tragic life of
Nietzsche was illustrative of the struggle of modern
man, torn between the destructive, Apollonian
forces of individuation and the life-giving, uniting
forces of Dionysian unity. In the religion of Dionysus we are able to "distinguish... the consciousness
of impersonal... spontaneity, the horror and ecstasy
of loss of self in chaos and of the new self-attain-
ment in God.... For the religion of Dionysus is a
mystical religion, and the soul of mysticism is the
idolization of man, through the beneficial approach
of the Deity to the human soul, which comes to
their total merging, or through an insight into the
true and intransient essence of the I...."[16] The real
meaning of Nietzsche's personal tragedy was that
"he understood the Dionysian source as an esthetic
one, and life as 'an esthetic phenomenon' "(p. 29).
But according to Ivanov, the Dionysian source is
"...above all a religious source, and the rainbows of

life's waterfall, to which Nietzsche's face was turned, are the refraction of the divine sun. If the Dionysian intoxication of life is only an esthetic phenomenon, then mankind is but an assembly [*sonm*] 'or craftsmen of Dionysus,' as antiquity called actors'' (p. 29).

Throughout all of Ivanov's complex, at times obtuse, but always sincere metaphysical conjecturing there is continually apparent his fervid belief that art, its practice and its influence, must have some greater essential meaning, some divine origin, through which it serves mankind.

Earlier in the same year, 1904, in an article entitled "The Poet and the Mob" ("Poet i chern' "),[17] Ivanov offered one of his clearest expositions of how art, through the medium of the poet, serves mankind. His point of departure is Pushkin's famous poem, "The Poet and the Crowd" ("Poet i tolpa"), which, in its most basic meaning, tells about the lack of communication between the poet and the crowd, the isolation of the poet and the seeming senselessness of his art with its "sweet sounds" in relation to the more practical contributions other segments of society make to the crowd's well-being. The poet's withdrawal from the crowd, according to Ivanov in "The Poet and the Mob," is "the fundamental fact of the soul's recent history, and the consequence of this fact is art's gravitation to esoteric isolation, refinement, the refinement of 'sweet sounds,' estrangement, the profundity of empty 'prayers.' The crowd forced the Poet to act upon it; his act was the refusal to act...." (p. 4). With Pushkin's vision as the prophecy, Ivanov moves to Tiutchev, who had been claimed as a predecessor by both the esthetes and the mystics within Russian Symbolism. He shows that Tiutchev was the first Russian "victim" of the new poetic "aphasia." He grew silent because "as with an electric spark, the Word is possible only in contact with the opposite poles of a single creation: [the poles of] artist and folk"

[95]

(p. 5). In other words, the significance of the new poetic silence, which is the fundamental feature of modern poetry, is that "the crowd has lost its organ of speech—the poet" (p. 5). Poetry's new condition is what led to the word's new function, the function of "indication," "hint," "symbol," for only "such a word [that is, a symbol] can not be a lie" (p. 6). This, of course, was the answer to Tiutchev's great insight, acknowledged as truth by Symbolists of every persuasion, that "a spoken thought is a lie" *("mysl' izrechennaia est' lozh' ").*

At this point there was no difference of opinion among the Symbolists as to why the symbol was the prime poetic vehicle. If, however, the symbol is not accessible to the crowd's understanding, the nature of art becomes even more esoteric, even more isolated; it becomes wholly individuated and loses its unifying purpose, religious or otherwise. This interpretation of the symbol in art is rejected by Ivanov. The symbol is not only the vehicle for inexpressible, incomprehensible thoughts; it also discloses in these thoughts "the petrified remains of ancient belief and idolizations, of forgotten myth and deserted cult" (p. 6). What Ivanov is driving at, what proves to be his link between the isolated poet and the crowd, is a sort of Jungian collective, mythic consciousness that only finds its expression (unconsciously) in the personal, but at the same time universal Symbolism of the poet: "...the poet's creation—and primarily that of the Symbolist poet—may be called an unconscious submersion into the elemental nature of folklore" (p. 7). Thus the poet loses his independent freedom of creation and becomes an unconscious instrument of the people's self-consciousness, an "organ of national memory" (p. 7). Now we are able to understand, according to Ivanov, that "true Symbolism must reconcile the Poet with the Crowd in a great, national art. The period of separation is passing. We are traveling the path of the symbol to the myth.

Great art is art that creates myth" (p. 8). The task
of the poet is clear, "for myth is the postulate of
the world's consciousness, and the Crowd, itself
not knowing what it wants, demanded myth from
the Poet" (p. 8).

Although Ivanov was to develop his theory in
depth and complexity over the course of the next
several years, its basic features were present as early
as 1904 in the articles just discussed, and it was precisely these elements of a greater, divine purpose of
art, of the artist's limited freedom, of myth creation,
neo-Populism, and religion that stood between
Ivanov and his followers on the one hand, and Briusov and his on the other. But before going on to
Briusov's rejection of Symbolism's mystically inclined adherents, we would do well to examine the
view of one of its most notable partisans, Aleksandr
Blok.

In a well-known article "On the Current Condition of Russian Symbolism" (O sovremennom sostoianii russkogo simvolizma"), Blok, calling himself
a "Baedeker" [18] for Ivanov's ideas, attempts to provide a clear exposition of the rival faction which
will show that there is "a reality hidden behind
[Ivanov's] words, which, at first glance, seem abstract" (p. 426). According to Blok, the initial recognition of a magic world, a world or worlds other
than the "objective" "real" world (as early perceived by Briusov and Sologub, for example), marks
the rise of a school. This is "the first youth, the
childish novelty of first discoveries" (pp. 426-27).
Maturity begins, however, when the Symbolist poet
recognizes that he is a "theurgist," "that is, the
possessor of secret knowledge, behind which there
is a mysterious activity" (p. 427). What happens
eventually to the poet-theurgist is that he "makes
his own life into art," that is, "life has become art"
(pp. 429-30). After life has been transformed into
art all the old barriers that had previously separated

Valery Briusov

the two no longer exist and there arise "...questions
of art's curse, of 'the return to life,' of 'civic service,'
of the church, of 'the people and the intelligentsia.'
[These questions are a] totally natural manifestation
that, of course, lies within the limits of Symbolism
...." (p. 431). Here, once again, we are able to see the
conflict arising, for art is no longer autonomous
(and according to Ivanov and Blok should not be so);
it has become so intimately involved with life that it
no longer has any identity of its own, and the poet—
art's instrument—has in essence ceased to be a poet
and has become a theurgist whose "secret knowledge"
involves him in all aspects of life in an almost extra-
literary sense.

If these, Blok's explanations, sound to us every
bit as abstract or mystical as those of Ivanov, it is
because we fail to realize that the Symbolist vision
pertains to the "objectivity" and "reality" of *"those
worlds"* (p. 431), that is, the worlds beyond our
own, to the secrets of which the Symbolist is privy.
For those who do not believe in the existence of the
other worlds, the Symbolists will seem to be "nothing
but Decadents, composers of unprecedented sensations, but who are speaking of death now only because they are tired" (p. 432). The implication here,
of course, is that the poets who profess to be Symbolists and do not believe in the existence of other
worlds (viz. Briusov and company) are themselves
"nothing but Decadents."

One of Briusov's most pointed refutations of
these divergent ideas was expressed in 1907 in a
polemical article directed against a piece by A. Gornfeld which had appeared in the newspaper *Comrade
(Tovarishch)*. Briusov's article, "The Victors' Triumph" ("Torzhestvo pobeditelei"),[19] served as a
point of departure for his analysis of the Symbolists'
new postures. We will see that Briusov has now
radically altered his conception of the nature of

literary schools. In the discussion of *On Art* above,
we pointed out the poet's insistence that "a school
of art only teaches external devices," and "the works
of the same school coincide with each other according to [these external, creative] devices," but *"can
be totally different one from another in terms of
content"* (p. 22, my italics). But now, in 1907, nine
years later, Briusov maintains that *"in no case is the
difference between schools of poetry a difference of
styles."*[20] To support this assertion he reminds his
readers that Novalis, Byron, Hugo, and Heine are all
considered Romantics, but by no stretch of the imagination can they be thought to have written in one
style (p. 55). Briusov now feels that the homogeneity
of a literary school lies rather in a *common world
view (mirosozertsanie).* The world view or principle
that has held the "Decadents" together as a literary
school (regardless of in what country they may have
written) is "extreme individualism" (p. 55).

There is more than one possible explanation
for Briusov's change of opinion in the question of
what makes a literary school. But all of these pos-
sibilities seem to rest on the same foundation—a
desire to maintain high standards in Russian poetry.
It is clear that Briusov had used both "Decadence"
and "Symbolism" for furthering his own career; but
since he felt that his own career was so closely tied
to the fortunes of Russian literary development in
general, one can hardly distinguish—indeed need
not—between his actions on behalf of himself and
those on behalf of Russian literature.

As shown above, he often publicly announced
his feelings that a school, in and of itself, is only in-
cidental to the growth of literature. Thus earlier,
when the only thing binding the Decadents together
was their unorthodox, shocking style, when they
were considered no more than rude, young upstarts,
it was just this style that they proclaimed to be
their distinguishing trait, or more exactly, the

distinguishing trait of poetry's advanced stage. Now, when "Decadence" had "conquered," when the "mob" was clamoring to read poets who had previously scorned its attention (this was the point of Gornfeld's article), Briusov maintains that Decadence is not what people think it is, even though it was primarily through him that the reading public received its understanding of the movement.

It appears, however, that Briusov in "The Victors' Triumph" was interested not so much in defining "Decadence" for the general reading public as in attacking the many deviant factions that were straying from the fold and trying to discredit the self-seeking hangers-on. When Briusov begins to speak in his article of the "schism" in Decadence as one between those who still maintain their "extreme individualism" and those who are striving to "overcome individualism" (p. 56), the polemical nature of the article becomes clear, especially if we consider the discussion earlier in this chapter of the ideas of Viacheslav Ivanov; and Briusov's apparent inconsistency, as noted above, loses its duplicity in the face of a much more persistent idea, namely that Decadence, Symbolism, or poetry in general is not and should not be at the service of mysticism or metaphysics: "Now one may ask: have the 'Decadents' preserved their former relation to individualism? No. It was precisely the question of individualism that was the point with which the split between the formerly 'united' school began. Thus, for example, the 'neo-Christians' were the first who moved away from the former nucleus of Decadence and sought a way in the Church to overcome individualism" (pp. 55-56).

Briusov was not attacking only those who had already split off from the camp; he was also laying out the basis for his coming battles with those who were still associated with *The Scales* and ostensibly still loyal to his ideas: "And as far as the world view of 'extreme individualism' truly survives the crisis, a differentiation [the word was Gornfeld's] in the midst of the 'Decadents' is inescapable. The inner contradictions of that world view, which recently seemed immutable, are exposed; the time of new reevaluations is coming, and because of this it is a time of division, of schism" (p. 56).

The extent of Briusov's "war"—with, in his opinion, the reactionary forces at work in literature—goes beyond a break with the splinter groups of neo-Christians and Mystical Anarchists (Chulkov's group, allied with Viacheslav Ivanov and Blok) on the one hand and dissenters within his own ranks on the other. There were still the newcomers to cope with, the "hooliganism" and "provocation" of the young, up-and-coming poets who "were never in a position to understand and interpret the significance of 'Decadence' " (p. 57).

Finally, and certainly most significantly, Briusov proclaimed the imminent death of Decadence. His strategy here is clear; by so doing he takes the ground out from under the feet of his enemies who are also using the banner of Decadence to legitimate themselves. As far as Briusov is concerned, he is now able to operate clear of the limits imposed by adherence to a specific school or group, a partial source of his discontent since 1905.

Briusov's proclamation of the demise of Decadence must be quoted in full, for it explicitly labels the forces of reaction against which Briusov felt he was defending the quality and integrity of Russian poetry, and it also explains what Briusov was looking forward to for poetry's future development:

"Decadence" is being differentiated, or more exactly, is dying: a quarter of a century is the age-limit for the life of a literary school; and "Decadence" has gone through it (counting from its first appearance in France in the beginning of the eighties). But "Decadence" can not yield its place to the naive advocates of muzzling in the Russian provinces, to the

hooligans who attribute to themselves the crucial name of
anarchists, or to light-hearted youths who think one does
not have to agonize over painful and unsolvable questions.
"Decadence" is waiting to give its scepter in the world of
art to a new group of artists who are connected to it in terms
of continuity. And if it is fated to close its eyes before the
emergence [of this new group] then it will answer, as did
Alexander the Great, the question of to whom to leave the
kingdom by saying: "To the most worthy" (p. 57).

Finally, in a postscript to his article, Briusov
makes it clear that he is no longer distinguishing between "Symbolism" and "Decadence," because
Symbolism "as a method of artistic creation" is
characteristic of all great artists in all periods and
that the Decadents only used it more than most
other schools. The fact that Briusov talks only of
Decadence in this article as far as a school is concerned and has ceased to treat Symbolism as one is
significant. *(The Scales'* "new" conception of Symbolism as opposed to Decadence will be discussed in
part two of this chapter.)

Thus, by the end of 1907, although he was still
to participate in *The Scales'* activities for a year,
Briusov had effectively isolated himself from the
journal which he had created. He made no new pacts
with any of the Modernist splinter groups, nor did
he begin any himself. He was alienated from his co-
workers at *The Scales,* and he had acknowledged that
Decadence was dying; but as far as his philosophy of
art was concerned, this "death" was a healthy development for literature.

For the final two years of *The Scales'* existence,
Briusov (although he continued to defend art's integrity in Russia from the pages of his journal) began
to branch out on his own and to expound more often
and more forcibly his non-aligned poetic creed.

2. The "Non-Theory" of Symbolism (1908)

In spite of all the personal differences Briusov might have had at various times with various members of *The Scales'* staff, he invariably went out of his way and gave in to them in order to keep *The Scales* free to engage the enemy's forces. These forces were extensive: *The Golden Fleece, The Divide, Torches* and the publishing house "Sweetbrier" ("Shipovnik"). Bely's memoirs, *The Beginning of The Century (Nachalo veka),* provide an excellent account of Briusov's relations with his fellow workers at *The Scales:* "...love of glory and love of power lived [in Briusov] ; but he dictated, so to speak, only in the humble provinces, as in [the various literary clubs and circles of Moscow] ; from the lecturn or from the stage: in his mother country, in the center of his circle of friends he behaved like a republican, as though he were with [fellow] warriors whom he helped in his time; we remembered this, and we were faithful to him...." [21]

Bely then relates how Briusov, in order not to drive his allies away from *The Scales,* often yielded to them in certain matters and allowed them to indulge themselves in ways he did not approve of. As an example, Bely notes that his own reviews on sociology in *The Scales* really did not fit the journal's "official program," but Briusov nevertheless allowed him to publish them (p. 161). By the end of 1907, however, there was no longer anyone on *The Scales'* staff whom Briusov could consider an ally. Even Andrei Bely, the only other Symbolist poet whose interest in versification and poetic theory approached Briusov's, was only a tactical ally, not a philosophical compatriot. As Briusov himself pointed out to Bely in 1907, their closeness was not due to any coincidence of ideas, but rather to the fact that they were both, each in his own way, "different" from all the others. [23]

Briusov's relationship with Bely during these

Valery Briusov

years provides a striking example of the singlemind-
edness of both men in literary matters. Although
their personal relations were strained to the utmost
as the result of a weird and grotesque love triangle,
they nevertheless cast off their personal enmity for
the sake of their literary battles.[24] Bely's account
of his association with Briusov after the beginning
of their personal confrontation attests to the
seriousness and dedication with which they approached their literary tasks:

[I] became [spiritually] bankrupt when the incident with
N. put me face to face with Briusov who had been the de-
fender of my literary aspirations, my tutor in the area of
style, my intellectual ally on the front in the struggle of
the Symbolists with academic routine.... If one considers
that in the fall of 1904 Briusov was jealous of N. and me,
and that in the beginning of 1905 he challenged me to a
duel, then one can imagine how I felt at *The Scales* left eye
to eye and not looking him in the eyes; we both, as best as
we were able, overcame ourselves for our common cause:
our work at *The Scales;* for we were being trumped in the
papers, in the journals, and at the Literary-Artistic Circle;
and I must say: under the flag of Symbolism we both
pushed through our personal enmity, at times even hatred,
whenever it was a matter of the fate of our literary movement, equally dear to us both.[25]

The "flag of Symbolism," however, had taken
on new colors since it had first appeared in Russia
under the title of *The Russian Symbolists.* In 1908
The Scales' polemical articles (and most of the
articles at this time were polemical), while directed
against groups not calling themselves Symbolist,
championed not a "Symbolist school," but an
esthetic method. In October, 1908, *The Scales*
published an article by Bely entitled "Symbolism
and Contemporary Russian Art" ("Simvolizm i sovremennoe russkoe iskusstvo"). In his exposition of
the difference between Symbolism and Modernism,

which, according to Bely were "confused" in the
minds of the critics,[26] he outlines all the various
schools and groups comprising the spectrum of Modernism in Russia. The spectrum is immense; it begins
with the Marxists and Realists (Gorky and *The Banner [Znamia]*) on the right. But even among the Realists there are those—Artsybashev and Kamensky, for
example—who do not belong to this group, but who
have adopted "some traits of cheap Nietzscheanism"
(p. 41). From here the line goes to the group
centered around "Sweetbrier," but this group in itself is so splintered and diverse that it too has a spectrum of adherents stretching from Realism through
Impressionism, to Symbolism, and back from Symbolism to Impressionism on its left flank. This latter
shift is to the schools of "Symbolic Realism" (or
"neo-Realism") and Mystical Anarchism (pp. 41-42).
The group of Mystical Anarchists *(The Scales* was
most concerned with this group) is, according to
Bely, "...the most complex and most motley group
of Modernists. Their ideology is a mixture of Baku-
nin, Marx, Solovyov, Maeterlinck, Nietzsche, and
even,... even Christ, Buddha, and Mohammed"
(p. 42). There are still additional groups of Modernists,
also quite complex. One was made up of "Merezhkovsky, Gippius, and the journalist-critics, Filosofov
and Berdiaev." "Then there is a group of writers who
are specifically working out the problems of religion;
Volzhsky, Bulgakov, Florensky, Sventsitsky, and
Ern" (p. 42). Finally in the field of "religious Modernism" there were still Lev Shestov and V. Rozanov
on the one hand and "Minsky's rather boring
'Meonism' " on the other (p. 42).

    Against all these groups and figures, against all
these new schools and philosophies, stands the group
of "actual" Symbolists, united around *The Scales*
and "the central figure of Valery Briusov" (p. 42).

    Here Bely gives a concise statement of what
Symbolism is and what it is not. The passage will be

Valery Briusov

quoted in its entirety, for it is one of the last statements in *The Scales* of the Symbolists' still imperfect and unformed creed. It is also of significance because it shows how close Bely and Briusov still were as far as their conception of the role of Symbolism in literature was concerned. Even though the lines were written by Bely, they are a distinct echo of Briusov's esthetic credo which will be expounded by him many times over in the future (long after Bely had gone over to the other side):

[The Symbolist group] rejects all hasty slogans about the overcoming or the interpretation of Symbolism. It is cognizant of the enormous responsibility that rests on Symbolism's theoreticians. It recognizes that the theory of Symbolism is the result of the multiferous work of all culture and that every theory of Symbolism that appears in our days, at best, is only the scheme of a plan by which the building will be constructed; conscientiousness in the building of a theory of Symbolism, the freedom of Symbolization—these are the slogans of this group (p. 42).

The summation of this passage is found further on in the article where Bely writes: "...for the present the theory of Symbolism still lies in the future" (p. 47). Much in the same way as Briusov had dealt with Decadence by declaring that it was dying, so, too, does Bely here knock the ground out from under *The Scales'* enemies by insisting that there is, as yet, no final theory of Symbolism. This puts the Scalesites in the position of being able to attack all the other esthetic theories propagated by their opponents while leaving their "non-theory" of Symbolism unassailable. The Briusov-Bely "non-theory" of Symbolism was not, however, only a tactical move. It expresses Briusov's final position in relation to Symbolism as an artistic method, and an artistic method is what Symbolism now was as far as Briusov (and Bely at this time) was concerned.

It had become customary for *The Scales* to

print an editorial statement of the journal's esthetic
position at the end of each year's publication. In
this statement for 1908, most likely written by
Briusov, much of Bely's above declaration is reprinted. At the same time the fundamental principles of Symbolism are further elaborated. Of importance is the handling of the question of individualism.

It will be remembered that in Briusov's article,
"The Victors' Triumph," he had stated that the
common denominator of the Decadents was "extreme individualism." One should also recall the
conspicuous absence of the word "Symbolism" in
relation to the "Decadent school." In *The Scales'*
statement for 1908, the strategy behind that move
becomes clear, for Briusov now removes Symbolism
from the question of individualism and thereby even
more completely divorces "the artistic method,
Symbolism" from any literary school. He then lays
the final stone by emphasizing the "non-theory" aspect of Symbolism's development:

We recognize unconditionally the independent value of art
as one of the highest manifestations of mankind. In art we
recognize Symbolism as the only true method of artistic
creation... But *The Scales* decisively separates the question
of Symbolism as a method of artistic creation from the
question of individualism. *The Scales* believes that that movement in art and literature which arose at the end of the
nineteenth century and is known under the name of "Symbolism" is still far from exhausted, and that the work of an
entire generation is still required in order to realize the tasks
mapped out by the first Symbolists.[27]

By stressing that the work of the "first" Symbolists
is neither exhausted nor completed, Briusov is clearly supporting Bely's position that there is, as yet, no
final theory of Symbolism.

After pointing out that this conception (or,
perhaps, non-conception) of Symbolism is the reason

Valery Briusov

for *The Scales'* attacks against those who either do not understand that Symbolism is the only true path of artistic development or those who wish to replace Symbolism with things that are "old hat." Briusov finally states conclusively that Symbolism is not *a partisan school:* "In any case, no matter how sharp our attacks upon other literary movements and other artists have been, these attacks have never been dictated by partisan intolerance" (p. 90).

The above remark, of course, is hardly true. The pages of *The Scales* are rife with attacks (particularly those directed against Georgy Chulkov, Viacheslav Ivanov, and the Mystical Anarchists) written by Briusov, Bely, and Ellis, as well as by others. These attacks are nothing less than vicious defamations in spite of the undoubtedly sincere reasons that inspired them.[28] The importance of the above quotation, however, lies in the fact that it shows, by its disclaiming any partisanship, the increasingly independent position assumed by *The Scales* and by Briusov. Therefore, it comes as no surprise that after he had declared "Decadence" dead and had forsworn any partisan adherence to Symbolism, Briusov left *The Scales* at the beginning of 1909.

3. The Death of *The Scales* (1909)

The question of how much Briusov's departure had to do with the fact that *The Scales* ceased publication the following year will probably never be definitively resolved. According to Maslenikov, it seems to have been a simple matter of cause and effect: "With his friend Briusov gone from its editorial staff, Poliakov, the 'angel' of the enterprise, probably felt that the costly periodical could be discontinued."[29] The answer, however, is considerably more complex than that. Two important factors are involved. The first concerns Briusov's entire attitude toward the journal and toward Symbolism; the second concerns Bely's reemerging sympathies for the ideas of Viacheslav Ivanov and Aleksandr Blok. Once again the need for objectivity becomes paramount. During Briusov's last two years with *The Scales,* he and Bely had acted as the journal's guiding forces. Bely supervised theoretical statements and attitudes while Briusov took care of literary criticism,[30] which included, of course, polemics against competing journals and publishing houses. Again, according to Maslenikov, Briusov was demoted while Bely received a promotion by the new arrangement of divided leadership.[31] This assertion, certainly not attested to in any sources, seems prompted by Maslenikov's negative attitude toward Briusov. He tells us that Briusov, "fearing to lose his own position as leader," and with his "supremacy" "threatened," "left all these matters [pertaining to theory] to Bely and gradually began to lose interest in the periodical" (p. 119). It would appear, however, perfectly consistent with Briusov's and Bely's previous attitudes, as well as with their roles in the journal up to this point, that they indeed turn to the tasks they did.[32] Briusov had little cause to fear losing his influence at *The Scales,* for he, more than any other member of that circle, had already attained national prominence with the publication of *Stephanos* in 1906 and not, as Maslenikov asserts, after 1909 when he joined the staff of *Russian Thought (Russkaia mysl').*[33]

Although the lines of difference between the members of *The Scales'* staff were clearly drawn—Bely, Poliakov (!), Baltrushaitis, and Likiardopulo against Briusov, Ellis, and S. Solovyov—these lines related only to the philosophical and metaphysical aspects of Symbolism and not to the real question of Symbolism as an artistic method. Bely tells us that even after the division, that is, after he was

charged with theory and Briusov with criticism, he
and Briusov together constituted a "third party"
(that is, in addition to the two groups mentioned
above) to engage in the common struggle against
the forces inimical to Symbolism.[34] For Bely the
opponent was Mystical Anarchism; for Briusov it
was any group that attempted to use Symbolism in
any context other than literary, specifically mystical or religious. Eventually Ellis and S. Solovyov,
ostensibly Briusov's allies at *The Scales,* joined with
Bely when the latter supported Ivanov and Blok in
the dispute between the "Clarists" and "Mystics."
But this did not happen until 1910.

There is further evidence that the split between Briusov and Bely at *The Scales* was not such
as to cause Briusov "to lose interest" and leave. For
one thing, the "theory" that became Bely's domain
was not the theory of versification, but philosophical theory, and, as Victor Erlich points out, "it was
fortunate indeed for the theory of Russian verse
that... Andrei Bely and Valery Briusov were... re-
markably conscious practitioners of the literary
craft. Their infinite knowledge of and vivid interest
in the problems of poetic techniques tempered to
a considerable extent their preoccupation with
'theurgy.' "[35] In this respect the differences separa-
ting Bely and Briusov were more of degree: they
were both theoreticians of poetry, but Briusov had
very little inclination toward metaphysics in the beginning while Bely did (one thinks of his venture with
Rudolf Steiner and anthroposophy). Later, by the
time Briusov left *The Scales,* he had lost any such
inclinations he may have had; Bely on the other
hand was by 1910 to become deeply involved with
metaphysics. There can be no doubt, however, that
Bely felt a fundamental affinity with Briusov in matters of personal disposition and temperament. He
expressed such feelings frequently: "It is exactly as
though Briusov grew up in my apartment. The

similarities are tremendous."[36] He continues to
point out the similarities in their childhood reading
and interests—they read the same philosophers—in
the games they played, in their love of the sciences,
and even in suffering the same kinds of delirium and
fantasies alone at night as boys.[37]

In his evaluation of Briusov's importance to
Russian poetry and the Symbolist movement Bely
goes even further than Briusov's Soviet defenders:
"Briusov is not only a great poet, he is our slogan,
our banner, our commander in the battle with routine and vulgarity *[poshlost']*."[38] And: "Valery
Briusov is the first among contemporary poets. His
name may be put only next to those of Pushkin,
Lermontov, Tiutchev, Fet, Nekrasov, and Baratynsky. He gave us models of eternal poetry. He taught
us anew to become aware of verse" (p. 178). Finally:
"Often he seems authoritative... But that authori-
tativeness comes from a feeling of responsibility. He
recognizes his responsibility for the fate of the movement that is dearer to him than life; and who among
us is so selflessly given over to his ideals?" (p. 199). It
is significant that this section of *The Green Meadow*
(Lug zelenyi) was written as late as 1908 and is not,
therefore, merely youthful exuberance on Bely's part.

Thus it seems clear that Bely and Briusov were
too close in their desires and aspirations to have
given up *The Scales* merely because of differences
in their world view, especially after they had overcome such personal hatred in working for the future
of Symbolism (see above). *The Scales* closed, as most
critics will agree, for a different reason: namely because it had attained its goal. That Briusov left a
year earlier is only evidence that he became aware of
this fact before his collaborators; that from *The*
Scales he went to what we today might call "esta-
blishment" journals is only evidence that he had decided to disavow partisan struggles and antagonisms
over metaphysical doctrine, which were, in his

opinion, useless. Metaphysics and religion were not literature, and literature was Briusov's life.

In its closing statement, "To Our Readers" ("K chitateliam"),[39] *The Scales* outlined why it was ceasing publication. There is no reason to doubt that Briusov agreed entirely with these conclusions: "...the reason motivating us to cease publishing *The Scales...* is the attainment of the goals we at one time set for it" (p. 186). The goals, of course, were two: "...advocacy of the new ideas and cultivation of young talent" (p. 189). And the result of attaining these goals was that *The Scales* "...created the 'Symbolist movement' in Russia, organized it, turned Symbolism from an object of scorn and rejection into an all-pervasive cultural phenomenon that is no longer rejected...." (p. 189).

The author of the article (most probably Bely himself) makes the important point that by this time—December, 1909—even those literary circles that displayed the most stubborn opposition to Symbolism at the time of its appearance now in one way or another have reacted to Symbolism's influence to such an extent that "their own literary physiognomy" is "unrecognizable" (p. 190). This is entirely correct. By the beginning of 1910 the Russian literary scene bore no resemblance to what it had been fifteen years before, and it is precisely for this reason that when Briusov left the Modernist circles per se, he was by no means returning to that milieu against which he had struggled so long. On the contrary, due to his inspiration and untiring leadership, the "respectable" segment of Russian literary society had been reformed to a point where it was no longer reactionary, but instead combined the finest traditions of Russia's literary past with the best, healthiest, most progressive elements of the new poetry. To a considerable extent, Briusov's literary battles from 1910 until the Revolution were directed against those forces which sought to pervert what might be called "healthy Symbolism" and transform it into an obscure mysticism. "To Our Readers" correctly predicted that now that Symbolism was omnipresent in Russian literature the immediate future of literature would revolve around what people were going to make of its new creed—Symbolism: "We do not mean... that the Symbolist movement has died, that Symbolism has ceased to play the role of an ideological slogan for our epoch.... But tomorrow the very same word [Symbolism] will become a different slogan...." (p. 191).

It is quite fitting that Bely refers to Symbolism as a "slogan" rather than "a school." For, as shown above, it was as a slogan, that is, a rallying point, that Briusov used it to pull Russian poetry up from the depths he felt it was in at the end of the nineteenth century. Interestingly enough, Bely too admitted years later that Symbolism was not a literary school as such; "...for Symbolism never thought itself to be a literary school: it was a 'school' from 1907 until 1909 for the sake of tactical considerations: for the struggle with cheap 'Mystical Anarchism'."[40]

After the closing of *The Scales* Briusov continued to use Symbolism as a *slogan* against the adherents of mysticism and religion in literature. For example, in his article, "On 'Slave Speech,' In Defense of Poetry" ("O 'rechi rabskoi', v zashchitu poezii"), Briusov makes his famous declaration that "...'Symbolism' *wanted to be and always was only art*" (original italics), and then reiterates his most consistently held belief: "Symbolism is a *method* of art, realized in that school which received the name 'Symbolistic.' By means of this, its method, art is differentiated from rationalistic cognition of the world in science and from extra-rational attempts to penetrate into [art's] secrets in mysticism. Art is autonomous; it has its own method and its own tasks" (original italics).[41] One cannot help but sense

a feeling of tired desperation in Briusov's impassioned
plea for the recognition of the truth he has been ex-
pounding: "But when will it be possible not to have
to repeat this truth that should have long since been
considered elementary! Is it possible that after art
was forced to serve science and civics they are now
going to force it to serve religion! Give it, finally, its
freedom!"[42]

Was Briusov correct in his struggles against the
forces that sought for so many years to make art
into something other than the autonomous method
of individual expression he always claimed it to be?
The rise of Acmeism in Russia and the subsequent
dominance of craftsmanship and impersonality in
Western poetry appear to support Briusov's life-
long esthetic posture. T. S. Eliot's definition of impersonality in poetry serves as an affirmation of the
truth in Briusov's quest for the proper application
of Symbolism in poetry, for it not only corroborates
Briusov's esthetic beliefs, it also describes the essential nature of his verse. "There are two forms of impersonality: that which is natural to the mere skill-
ful craftsman, and that which is more and more
achieved by the maturing artist.... The second impersonality is that of the poet who, out of intense and
personal experience, is able to express a general
truth; retaining all the particularity of his experience,
to make of it a general symbol."[43]

4. The End of Symbolism (1909-1910)

The beginning of the end of Russian Symbolism
is usually considered by most literary historians to
be 1909-1910.[44] In 1910, the year after *The Scales*
ceased publication, *The Golden Fleece* closed its
presses as well. *The Divide* had stopped publishing
in 1907. Among the miscellanies, *Torches'* last issue
appeared in 1908 and *Northern Flowers'* in 1911.
Only *Apollon (Apollo)* survived after Symbolism's

collapse to become the organ of the Acmeists and
continued to publish until 1917. Bely's own realization of Symbolism's failure, according to Maslenikov, was characteristic of the movement's dis-
integration in general, for "when others who had
believed in Symbolism as a way of life, as a revelation of the truth, realized that their prophet had
failed them, they necessarily rejected Symbolism as
an infallible philosophy. Thus the crisis in Bely's life
also played an important role in the crisis that developed in Symbolism, which soon spelled the doom of
the movement."[45] On the other hand, as Briusov had
pointed out earlier, twenty-five years is long enough
for any movement. Briusov, for one, certainly felt that
Symbolism was dying a natural death. In a newspaper
interview given to A. Izmailov in 1910, Briusov expressed certain thoughts on the passing of Symbolism that show his continued understanding of the
era as a step on a greater road. His thoughts on the
passing of Symbolism were certainly shared by many
of his more objective contemporaries:

At one time it was all very nice and perhaps even necessary.
Now it is just as impossible for us to return to it as it is for an
adult to return to his childhood toys. Some adjective, for
example, "kissy" *[potseluinyi]* was at that time new and
appropriate, because it was said for the first time. But if I
were to see it in a poem that appeared yesterday, I would
somehow feel uncomfortable for the author's sake. That has
all passed. One can no longer remain with the previous form,
otherwise one will seem silly. A year ago I left *The Scales*
precisely because I felt how outdated, what a backward
phenomenon their faith had become.[46]

Both the fact that those who believed in Symbolism as a type of panacea became disillusioned
and the fact that literary movements die natural
deaths and become outdated are significant for the
decline of Symbolism. By the same token, the fact
that Briusov ceased his efforts to keep the movement

Valery Briusov

"pure" by serving as its leader played just as significant a role in the transition from Symbolism to
Acmeism as did the other factors already mentioned.
One must also keep in mind the rather paradoxical
fact that it was actually the success of Symbolism
which helped create the crisis in which the movement found itself at the beginning of the second
decade of the twentieth century. When Symbolism
became "respectable," epigonous poets, most of
them endowed with little or no talent, rushed to
climb on the band wagon, and with their appearance
the nature of the movement of necessity changed.

Seen from a larger perspective—and here Briusov's vision was keen—Russian literature, or more
precisely, Symbolism, was suffering the same fate
that had befallen Russian literature in the eighties.
The freshness that had accompanied the first appearance of the Symbolists—at a time when literature was subordinate to extra-literary ideas—had become stagnant. And now, the leading practitioners
of Symbolism (with the exception, of course, of
Briusov and later Blok as well) were engaged in an
effort to subordinate literature once again to the
other extra-literary ideas, this time primarily to
religious rather than civic ones. It was the overwhelming desire on the part of those poets inclined
toward mysticism and religion to find in Symbolism
refuge and vindication for their philosophical beliefs
that more than anything else brought about the fall
of the movement. In Russia Symbolism in literature
was conceived and nurtured as a means of *literary*
expression. Of course there were philosophical overtones, as there are with every esthetic system, but
once these philosophical overtones became dominant, once the conception of Symbolism as a means
to greater literature was lost sight of or ignored, the
movement ceased to have any reason to exist.

In a famous letter written in March, 1910, (the
same month as the above interview) Briusov gave a

striking picture of the state of Russian letters from
his point of view:

Russia, they say, is tired—tired from war, from the revolution, from Decadence, from pornography... from everything....
No one wants books anymore, and not only "Skorpion editions" but any edition. There is panic in the book market
(...two ruble editions are now going for ten kopecks!). In
criticism there was only Kornei [Chukovsky], and now he is
in disgrace with a good half of his readers. For that matter
there are hardly any writers left; you can count them on
your fingers. Merezhkovsky is repeating himself hopelessly;
Z. N. Gippius has "finished blossoming" (as Balmont says);
Minsky has fallen lower than the lowest; Sologub has become famous; Balmont has written himself out for good;
Bely composed *The Silver Dove;* Blok is writing about the
intelligentsia. Who else is there!...
    In our circle, among the ex-Decadents, there is a great
schism: the fight of the "Clarists" with the "Mystics." The
Clarists belong to *Apollo:* Kuzmin, Makovsky, and others.
The Mystics belong to the Moscow [publishing house]
"Musaget": Bely, Viacheslav Ivanov, S. Solovyov, and others.
Essentially the ancient decrepit controversy over "free" art
and tendentiousness has been resumed. The "Clarists" defend clarity, clarity of thought, idiom, and images, but this
is only form; and in actuality they are defending "poetry
the goal of which is poetry," as old man Ivan Sergeevich
[Turgenev] said. The "Mystics" preach "renovated Symbolism,"
"myth creation" *[mifotvorchestvo]*, and the like; and in
actuality they want poetry to serve their Christianity, that
it become *ancilla theologiae.* Recently at a meeting of "Free
Esthetics" we had a great battle about this. The result, it
seems, is such that "Musaget" has definitely separated from
"Skorpion" (intellectually). I am, as you guess, with the
"Clarists" with all my heart.[47]

It comes as no surprise that Briusov sided so
strongly with the "Clarists," that is, with the soon-
to-be Acmeists, for Acmeism, at least in its initial
form and according to its manifesto, was little more
than Briusov's own brand of Symbolism.

Valery Briusov

In retrospect we often note that there was no essential difference between the Acmeists and the Symbolists; and this is correct if we understand Symbolism in the sense that we usually do when we speak of the "Moscow Symbolists" or the "first generation of Symbolists." In this light Briusov's review of Nikolai Gumilev's early collection of verse *Romantic Flowers (Romanticheskie tsvety)* is of interest. The review would be of note if it were only for the fact that it was highly favorable (Briusov rarely gave favorable reviews to new poets), but more significant and telling is the fact that Briusov sees in Gumilev's poetry certain traits that are obviously similar to his own, traits that were eventually to become the proclaimed hallmarks of Acmeist poetry. Briusov singles out the grace and interesting "form" of the young poet's verses. He calls Gumilev "a serious worker" (surely one of the highest compliments Briusov could pay a poet) who knows what he wants and knows how to obtain it.[48] Of particular interest is Briusov's admiration for Gumilev's impersonality, for the infrequency of the first-person pronoun, for the slightly Parnassian flavor of his verse, and for the subject matter, especially Gumilev's ventures into past centuries.[49] That Briusov should express admiration for some of the most characteristic traits of his own poetry was neither unusual nor significant. It was of significance, however, that these traits, so much a part of Briusovian poetry and esthetics, were to become characteristic for the next generation of Russian Modernists.[50]

It was to be another two years or so before Acmeism reached its zenith. In the meantime, however, there was a literary interregnum, for by this time Symbolism as a "school" was irreparably damaged and divided. Although its influence was to continue to be felt until the Soviets squashed it totally, Symbolism cannot be termed a cohesive movement after the closing of *The Scales* in 1909

or, at the latest, after the battle between the "Clarists"
and "Mystics" in 1910.

Much of the rest of Briusov's creative life may
be seen as an attempt to find the proper new idiom
to express himself. That he never succeeded in finding a proper niche for himself in Russian literature
after 1910 was his greatest tragedy, for he was acutely aware of the necessity for so doing. It is as though
T. S. Eliot had Briusov in mind when he wrote:
"...but it is my experience that towards middle age
a man has three choices: to stop writing altogether,
to repeat himself with perhaps an increasing skill of
virtuosity, or by taking thought to adapt himself to
middle age and find a different way of working."[51]
The first choice was unthinkable for a man like Briusov to whom work was life itself. The second
choice could have been taken from the reviews of
Briusov's subsequent collections of poetry.[52] And
it was because he realized that he was doing no more
than playing variations on an old theme that Briusov
made his last, futile efforts to become attuned to
the new voices in Russian poetry, voices which, for
the most part, had learned their scales from the
master but had by now far outdistanced him. His
attempts to write "scientific poetry" *[nauchnaia
poeziia]* were dismal failures. In later life—that is,
after the Revolution—Briusov achieved success in
the role for which he had always been best suited,
that of the brilliant teacher of poets more talented
than himself.

5. Briusov's Last Years (1910-1924)

Once Briusov left the ranks of the Russian
Symbolists and ceased his active participation in
the battles and polemics that continued to take
place after 1910, particularly the struggles between
the old guard and the emerging group of Acmeists,
the emphasis in Briusov's literary activities may be

said—in very general terms, of course—to have switched from poetry to teaching.

He continued to write, of course, and indeed every bit as much as before. But in addition to his collections of poems, his short stories, novels, and critical essays, he began more and more frequently to engage in what one can only call academic activities. In 1914, for example, he allowed himself the time to work extensively on his translation of Virgil's *Aeneid,* a project on which he had worked on and off for more than fifteen years. Around the same time he began his almost legendary adventures with Armenian poetry, which resulted in his monumental translations of the landmarks of the Armenian poetic art from its beginnings until modern times—this after having learned the language in one year! The many instructional texts on versification already mentioned were written between 1918 and his death.

It was after the Revolution, however, that Briusov assumed the role of literary bureaucrat and academician in a more formal sense, for shortly after 1917 he began his association with the *Narkompros,* and a long series of various literary positions followed. From 1918 through 1919 he was the manager of *Narkompros'* Division of Scientific Libraries; in 1919 he served in the State Publishing House; in 1920, the same year in which he joined the Communist Party, he organized the so-called *LITO* (Literary Division of *Narkompros).* *LITO* was officially characterized as the "regulatory organ of the nation's literary life."[53] The jobs in various bureaus and commissions continued for the rest of Briusov's life. In the constant changing from position to position, from professorship to professorship, one can sense the obvious dilemma which confronts the "extreme individualist" who attempts in vain to stifle his individualism and egotism and to subordinate his own interests and career to the will of the people, as the expression went. His attempts at this, however, were hardly successful, particularly psycho-logically, and the man who devoted the greater part of his life to the cause of culture spent his waning years watching culture being recast into mass con-formity and elementary literacy.

After eight years of frustrated seeking, Briusov died on October 9, 1924, in Moscow, of membranous pneumonia and pleurisy.

CONCLUSION

Valery Briusov's life and literary activities chronicle an era and provide important insights into the fundamental nature of Russian Symbolism. If Symbolism is an integral part of a greater unity, as Professor Chizhevskij claims (see above), it is nevertheless distinct from the rest of Modernism. Whereas Acmeism was born of a native brand of Symbolism, Russian Symbolism itself began as the offspring of a foreign trend, the new poetry of France, and ended by combining the most enduring traits of its French predecessor with those of its own magnificent poetic heritage, the heritage of Pushkin, Baratynsky, Lermontov, Tiutchev, and Fet. For both its initial as well as its final form, Russian Modernism is deeply indebted to Valery Briusov.

Were it not for Briusov's efforts and singular personality the development of Russian Symbolism would undoubtedly have followed a radically different course from that which it finally took. The fundamental trends were, of course, already present on the Russian literary scene before Briusov's appearance. The literary public knew the mystical, philosophical religiosity of D. Merezhkovsky's verse and the wild, unfettered "art for art's sake" of K. Balmont's poetry. It is possible that either one of these trends could have attained, for a time, ascendancy in Russian poetry. It is even more likely, however, that the 1890s and 1900s in Russia would have seen a series of poets appear and disappear, most of them leaving no trace of their art and a few leaving shining stars of brilliant verse against a monotonous, gray firmament of mediocrity. Even if there had been no Briusov, there would have been Bely, Blok, and Sologub, S. Solovyov, Ellis, and Z. Gippius. But it is doubtful if these poets would ever have attained the public forum and respect they did in such a short time if Briusov had not put his tremendous

organizational talents and devotion to art at the
service of the "new ideas." More than anything else
it was Briusov's own personality and nature, his
deep and enduring love for culture and learning, his
realistic attitude toward life and art, his erudition,
his appreciation for sound, well-founded, innovative poetry, and his high esteem for the history of
the literary tradition that enabled him to shape the
course of Russian poetry and esthetics to the extent
he did.

But all of these admirable characteristics required the more eccentric, egotistical quirks of his
personality—at times more than unpleasant—as a
catalyst, for were it not for his curious drive "to be
first," his vague dreams of "glory" and "fame,"
manifest in his childhood, there would not have
been the first, shocking collection of *The Russian
Symbolists,* there would not have been the letters,
articles and debates, the recruiting, polemics, and
esprit that represented the labor pains of the incipient movement. By the same token it was Briusov's curiously "unpoetlike" disposition toward
science and mathematics, toward scholarship, painstaking study and craftsmanship that preserved the
movement from the inevitable chaos of mysticism
and uncontrolled experimentation that threatened
it from the very beginning. Briusov brought the
clear, cold, hard stability of literary Classicism to his
frenzied neo-Romantic age in much the same way
that Pushkin, admired by Briusov above all other
Russian poets, exerted the stabilizing influence of
his careful craftsmanship upon his own epoch. Just
as Spinoza, whom Briusov studied intensely in his
youth, tried to create an anthropological philosophy
"which is free from the errors and prejudices of a
merely anthropocentric system," and a "mathematical theory of the moral world,"[1] so too did Briusov
entertain the thought of creating an esthetic philosophy free from the errors and prejudices of

Valery Briusov

Romantic intuition and mystical religiosity, a poetics that would aspire to mathematical certainty in the matter of poetry's progressive advance to higher levels of attainment.

Briusov's impact on the development of Russian Symbolism, however, is as difficult to assess in all its ramifications as it is unmistakable. There is, for one thing, the matter of his influence on two of Russia's greatest poets, Aleksandr Blok and Andrei Bely, both of whom have openly acknowledged their indebtedness to the older poet. But this influence is so extensive as to make it impossible to measure accurately. It includes such intangibles as inspiration, example, and support, poetic technique, subject matter, and education. By means of hundreds of translations, extensive articles, and reviews of the poetry of Western Europe, Briusov introduced an entire generation of Russian poets to many generations of foreign artists. Who can ever tell how far reaching the results of these labors were? Through well over two hundred articles, reviews and editions of the works of Russia's leading nineteenth-century poets, Briusov led an entire generation of Russian artists to understand and cherish the Russian literary heritage, and by the example of his own poetry he showed them how to utilize this heritage.

In this light, comments by N. Gumilev show vividly the instructive power of Briusov's example on his fellow artists. At the same time, Gumilev suggests a reason (other than political) for the widespread enmity so often directed against Briusov:

Probably no single contemporary poet has been written about as much as Valery Briusov; probably never have so many representatives of so many varied [literary] movements become angry at anyone as much as they have at Briusov. One must admit that they have all had cause to do so, for Briusov had lured all of them, each in his turn, with the hope of calling him their own; and having lured them, he slipped away. But nevertheless, it is strange, for we do not perceive his work as a conglomerate of poems all different one from another, but, to the contrary, his work appears to us to be a whole, harmonious and indivisible. This is not eclecticism: the distinguishing feature of Briusov's themes is rather in severe poverty than in senseless diversity.... It is not surprising that the words "the Briusovian school" sound just as natural and understandable as the Parnassian or Romantic schools. Truly, a conqueror but not an adventurist, careful but decisive too, calculating but in the same way as a brilliant strategist, Valery Briusov has made the characteristic traits of all the former literary schools his own.... But he has added something to them that has caused them to begin to burn with a new fire.... Perhaps this something is the basis of the new school that is coming to take Symbolism's place; for Andrei Bely has said that Briusov transmits his commandments through the heads of his contemporaries.[2]

In this statement lies the key to Briusov's impact on Russian Modernism. Much of its finest poetry displays the mark of the "Briusovian school," and this mark signifies the incorporation into the new poetry of "the characteristic traits of all the former literary schools" with the addition of the poet's individual genius. It is this last element that prevents poetry, which has taken cognizance of tradition, from being eclectic or merely imitative.

In this respect Briusov's esthetic theory again brings to mind that of T. S. Eliot, particularly as expressed in the essay "Tradition and the Individual Talent." In this essay Eliot exhorts the poet to incorporate the experience of the poetic tradition into his own work, to "develop or procure the consciousness of the past... [and to] continue to develop this consciousness throughout his career."[3] It is the sense of history, according to Eliot, which the poet brings to his own time and place, that makes him "most acutely conscious of his place in time, of his own contemporaneity" (p. 14). In *Experiments* which is the result of six years of poetic experimentation based on past traditions of versification,

Valery Briusov

Briusov writes: "The task of every poet—along with his creative work, which remains, of course, the chief task of his entire life—is as much as possible to facilitate the development of the technique of his art; *to search, to repeat that which has been found by others, applying it to his own language and to his own time,* to make experiments—here is one of the most important tasks before the poet if he wants to work not only for himself, but for others as well and for the future."[4]

It is to Briusov's everlasting credit that he, more than anyone else, brought this message home to the Symbolists, who in turn passed it on to the next generation of Russian Modernists. With his awareness of the power of tradition, Briusov was able to transform Modernism from a movement that was perceived by his contemporaries as retrogressive, chaotic, and destructive into something they were able to recognize as a "re-creation of tradition" (the phrase is Eliot's).

From the preceding study of Briusov's career it is clear that he had an abiding concern for the poet's image, one almost as great as his concern for poetry itself. It is most likely because of Briusov's overwhelming interest in the poet as such that Victor Erlich found him suitable for his study in *The Double Image.* This regard for the figure of the poet, however, proved yet another way for Briusov to raise the stature of modern poetry in Russia to the position he felt it deserved. In an article entitled "Viacheslav Ivanov and Andrei Bely," Briusov wrote: "Only in his own days was Pushkin's great authority able to convince all society that poetry was a necessary and important matter and that the works of the poets deserve attention and sympathy.... When, in the West... first the Romantics, then the Parnassians, and finally the Symbolists labored over [artistic technique], in Russia each poet worked alone, at his own risk."[5] When thought of in light of the above, it appears that Briusov's exhausting efforts at the beginning of the century to recruit poets into a cohesive unit or "school" and to assume firm leadership over this group were made much more for the common cause of art than for mere self-aggrandizement (although self-aggrandizement was undoubtedly part of his motivation). Without this cohesive unity and the awareness of the work, the achievements, and the failures of fellow poets, both in Russia and abroad, the artistic accomplishments of the Modernistic epoch in Russian poetry would certainly have been considerably less. According to D. S. Mirsky, precisely the elevation of the poet per se was an indispensible task for Briusov and his generation: "It was necessary to raise the poet's calling, to return to him his priest's position...."[6]

Ultimately Briusov's greatest contribution to the history of Russian literature, a contribution for which he has been denied adequate recognition and appreciation, was his ceaseless effort to raise the poet, poetry, and culture in general to a point where they could exert their civilizing influence on a chaotic and desperate world. Whether practical or impractical, the vision was a noble one and the effort heroic.

NOTES

INTRODUCTION

1. P. S. Kogan, *"Literaturnye napravleniia i kritika 80-kh i 90-kh godov,"* in *Istoriia russkoi literatury XIX v.,* Vol. V, ed. D. N. Ovsianiko-Kulikovskii (M. 1911), 66.

2. Dmitrij Tschizhewskii, *Vergleichende Geschichte der slavischen Literaturen,* Vol. II (Berlin, 1968), 78.

3. Kogan, *"Literaturnye napravleniia,"* 74.

4. *Novaia russkaia poeziia* (Berlin, 1923), 7.

5. Kogan, *"Literaturnye napravleniia,"* 65.

6. Adolf Stender-Petersen, *Geschichte der russischen Literatur,* Vol. II (Munich, 1957), 508.

7. *O prichinakh upadka i o novykh techeniiakh sovremennoi russkoi literatury,* excerpted in *Literaturnye manifesty,* ed. N. L. Brodskii *et al.* (M. 1929), 10-11.

8. Kogan, *"Literaturnye napravleniia,"* 99-100.

CHAPTER I

1. For this general discussion of Briusov's youth I have drawn upon the following biographical sources: N. Ashukin, *Valerii Briusov v avtobiograficheskikh zapisiakh, pis'makh, vospominaniiakh sovremennikov i otzyvakh kritiki* (M. 1929); hereafter referred to as Ashukin. Valerii Briusov, *"Avtobiografiia,"* in *Istoriia russkoi literatury XX veka,* Vol. I, ed. S. A. Vengerov (M. 1914), 101-118; hereafter referred to as *"Avtobiografiia."* Valerii Briusov, *"Kratkaia avtobiografiia,"* in *Valeriiu Briusovu. Sbornik statei posviashchennyi 50-tiletiiu so dnia rozhdeniia poeta,* ed. P. S. Kogan (M. 1924), 13-15; hereafter referred to as *"Kratkaia avtobiografiia."* Valerii Briusov, *Iz moei zhizni. Moia Yunost'. Pamiati,* ed. N. Ashukin (M. 1927); hereafter, referred to as *Iz moei zhizni.* Ioanna Briusova, *"Materialy k biografii Valeriia Briusova,"* in Valerii Briusov, *Izbrannye stikhi,* ed. Igor Postupal'skii (M. 1933), 119-49; hereafter referred to as *"Materialy."*

2. B. Vnuchkov, *"Dva pis'ma V. Ya. Briusova," Moskva* (November, 1969), 193.

3. *"Avtobiografiia,"* 102.

4. *Ibid.,* 103.

5. *Iz moei zhizni,* 16.

6. *"Avtobiografiia,"* 103.

7. "Reminiscences of N. Ya. Briusova," in "Materialy," 121.

8. *Ibid.*

9. N. Gudzii, *"Iunosheskoe tvorchestvo Briusova,"* in *Literaturnoe nasledstvo,* Vols. 27-28 (M. 1937), 202.

10. Ashukin, 23.

11. *Iz moei zhizni,* 24-25. Incidents such as these occurred frequently in Briusov's childhood. As a man, Briusov was to be attacked for his personality more often than for his poetry—or rather, his personality was to be used as a basis for attacks on his poetry. Thus, in referring to the event just described, Konstantin Mochulsky, in his

book *Valerii Briusov* (Paris, 1962, 17-18), writes: "Briusov's childhood was severe and joyless. He had no companions, he knew no
fairy tales, he was unable to play, he was morose and unsociable.
'The boys did not like to play with me,' the poet admits, 'the more
so because I wanted *to take precedence.'* Sickly self-esteem and
vanity appeared in him from early childhood. Once the six-year-old
boy fought with a comrade and was beaten, climbed into a tree and
sat there for a long time contemplating a plan for suicide: he even
composed a suicide note. He considered suicide often, at every col-
lision with reality." The author's rhetoric and irony in the above
passage makes his attitude toward Briusov the man (an attitude which
becomes more pronounced in relation to the poet's personal life as
the book progresses) quite clear. In general, any biographer of Briusov
must be careful in judging personal evaluations of the poet by those
who knew him. Very often these evaluations are colored more by
bitterness at Briusov's having become a member of the Communist
Party than by any rational considerations. Thus, the emigrés, Khodasevich, Mochulsky, and Tsvetaeva, for example, write devastatingly
concerning Briusov the man as well as Briusov the poet. On the other
hand, Bely and Blok, both of whom had more than ample reason to
dislike Briusov personally, continually lauded him as a poet.

12. *Iz moei zhizni,* 17. Subsequent references to this work will
be given in the text.

13. Many of these early sketches as well as later ones are repro-
duced on the pages of *Literaturnoe nasledstvo,* Vols. 27-28.

14. Briusov also carried his interest in betting to school where
he organized a pari-mutuel gate based on the results of the teachers'
speeds in reaching their respective classes on the third floor. The
venture was quite successful. *Iz moei zhizni,* 51-52.

15. See Andrei Bely's account of the effect of Polivanov's on
Briusov: "The Polivanov period stopped Briusov's vulgarity short. I
think this was the influence of the Gymnasium. In the first place,
there was the composition of the student body; Briusov was tied to
some of them in a cultural relationship (this was not so at Kreiman's);
Briusov began to live life at the Gymnasium.... From Briusov's [diary]
as a student it is apparent that his interests were attuned to those
of the class; and this youthful cultural collective was in turn attuned
to the faculty" *(Na rubezhe dvukh stoletii* [Chicago, 1966], 294).

16. *Ibid.*

17. "*Avtobiografiia,*" 107.

18. "*Materialy,*" 122.

19. Gudzii, "*Iunosheskoe tvorchestvo,*" 202.

20. *Polnoe sobranie sochinenii i perevodov,* Vol. I: *Iunosheskie
stikhotvoreniia. Chefs d'Oeuvre. Me eum esse. (Stikhi 1892-1899 gg.)*
(St. Petersburg, 1913), ix. In addition to Vol. I, the only other volumes of
Briusov's projected twenty-five volume complete works to be published were the following: XII-1913; XIII-1913; II-1914; III-1914; XV-
1914; IV-1914; XXI-1914. Henceforth this collection will be referred
to as *Complete Works.*

21. Gudzii, "*Iunosheskoe tvorchestvo,*" 202.

22. *Ibid.,* 203-04.

23. *Ibid.,* 210.

24. *Iz moei zhizni,* 76.

25. "*Avtobiografiia,*" 107.

26. See also D. Maksimov, *Poeziia Valeriia Briusova* (L. 1940), 35-36, and Georgette Donchin, *The Influence of French Symbolism on Russian Poetry* (The Hague, 1958), 11-12.

27. Zinaida Vengerova, *"Poety simvolisty vo Frantsii: Verlen, Mallarme, Rimbo, Laforg, Moreas,"* *Vestnik Evropy* (September, 1892), 143.

28. Valerii Briusov, *Dnevniki: 1891-1910,* ed. I. M. Briusova and N. S. Ashukin (Moscow, 1927), 12. Subsequent references to this work will be given in the text.

29. *Dnevniki,* 13. Actually Polivanov's Gymnasium may be seen in retrospect as having been the breeding ground for the future Symbolists. In *Na rubezhe dvukh stoletii* Bely writes: "If someone were to have told Polivanov in 1895 that his dear, highly valued and close acquaintance, Lev Lvovich Kobylinsky... would hurt him twice (first by Marxism, second by Symbolism) under the pseudonym of Ellis, that his pupils Bugaev and S. M. Solovyov, to whom he was attentive, were also to become 'Symbolists,' uniting around Briusov, he would have groaned... and just at that time Briusov finished the Gymnasium while preaching Symbolism to Yasiuninsky, Inoev, Yakovlev, and Shcherbatov (and they took it up); that is, the eighth form (about which Polivanov wrote Nikolsky that this class 'is such a charming one') already contained 'venom' in its highest interests, and dangerous 'venom'... The future Polivanov 'Decadents'...were nevertheless carriers of that disease which soon caused the enlightened teacher of Areopagus to groan" (321-22).

30. Quoted in Ashukin, 55.

CHAPTER II

1. "*Avtobiografiia,*" 109-10.

2. August, 1894, 890-92; January, 1895, 421-24; October, 1895, 847-51.

3. *Complete Works,* I, 7.

> *Zolotistye fei*
> *V atlasnom sadu!*
> *Kogda ia naidu*
> *Ledianye allei?*
>
> *Vliublennykh naiad*
> *Serebristye vspleski!*
> *Gde revnivye doski*
> *Vam put ' pregriat'?*
>
> *Neponiatnye vasy*
> *Ognem ozaria,*
> *Zastyla zaria*
> *Nad poletom fantazii.*

Za mrakom zaves
Pogrebal'nye urny,
I ne zhdet svod lazurnyi
Obmanchivykh zvezd.

4. *Vestnik Evropy* (August, 1894), 892.
5. Quoted in Ashukin, 59-60.
6. *Russkaia literatura kontsa XIX-nachala XX v.,* ed. B. A. Bialik *et al.* (M. 1968), 310.
7. *Ibid.,* 315.
8. *Vestnik Evropy* (January, 1895), 423.

V serebrianoi·pyli polunochnaia vlaga
Pleniæt otdykhom ustalye mechty,
I v zybkoi tishine rechnogo sarko·faga
Velikii chelovek ne *slyshit klevety.*

It is of rather ironic interest that in 1894 K. Medvedsky in an article entitled "Symbolism on Russian Soil" *("Simvolizm na russkoi pochve")* wrote of Solovyov, whom he called "This first Russian Symbolist": "This work *[The White Lily]* is unconditionâlly pathological and the creative thought of a normal man did not participate in it." *Nabliudatel'* (January), 331.
9. *Russkoe bogatstvo* (October, 1895). Quoted in Bialik, *Russkaia literatura,* 331.
10. October, 1895, 849.
11. Quoted in Bialik, *Russkaia literatura,* 375.
12. "Valerii Briusov," in *Arkhaisty i novatory* (L. 1929), 526.
13. Bialik, *Russkaia literatura,* 332.
14. The "Interview" has been republished in K. Loks, *"Briusov-teoretik simvolizma," Literaturnoe nasledstvo,* Vols. 27-28, 265-75.
15. *Ibid.,* 268.
16. By "your article" Briusov means Arsenii G., *"Moskovskie simvolisty"* ("The Moscow Symbolists"), *News of the Day,* August 29, 1894. It should be noted that Briusov's distinction between Petersburg and Moscow factions, a distinction generally considered valid even today, deserves qualification in regard to various figures of the Symbolist movement and various times in the movement's history. For a discussion of these qualifications see Renato Poggioli, *The Poets of Russia: 1890-1930* (Cambridge, Mass, 1960), 57-58. Aleksandr Mikhailovich Dobroliubov, 1876-1944 (?), was one of the earliest St. Petersburg decadents. His books *(Natura naturans. Natura naturata,* 1895, *Sobranie stikhov,* 1900, and *Iz knigi nevidimoi,* 1905) are among the most interesting examples of Russian Decadent poetry. Shortly after the appearance of his first book. Dobroliubov set out to wander across the face of Russia preaching his own sectarian religion based on a sort of Christian universal brotherhood.
17. In 1895 Pertsov included one of Briusov's poems in his anthology *Young Poetry (Molodaia poeziia).*

18. See Briusov's perceptive discussions of Minsky and Mere-zhkovsky in *The Far and Near Ones (Dalekie i blizkie)*, (M. 1912), 46-53 and 54-64.

19. Unpublished note made by Briusov in 1895. Quoted in N. Gudzii, *"Iz istorii rannego russkogo simvolizma," Iskusstvo* (April, 1928), 218.

20. T. Ardov, *Otrazheniia lichnosti. Kriticheskie opyty* (M. 1909). Quoted in Ashukin, 92.

21. *The Poets of Russia*, 105.

22. Quoted in Ashukin, 101.

23. *Ibid.*, 98.

24. *Dnevniki*, 22.

25. *"Avtobiografiia,"* 110. A leading Briusov scholar, D. Mak-simov, concurs with Briusov's own estimation of *Chefs d'Oeuvre:* "The width of Briusov's range (in part even in his early work) is astounding. Even the first independent collection of Briusov's poems, *Chefs d'Oeuvre* (1895, particularly the 2nd edition of 1896) cannot be reproached for monotony of lyrical themes. And in its generic varia-tions, lyric *tonalities,* forms, strophes, and meters it is undoubtedly richer than many similar collections of that time." *Poeziia Valeriia Briusova*, 26.

26. *"Avtobiografiia,"* 110.

27. L. A. de Bogdanovitch told the English readers of *The Athenaeum* in 1897 that "...the reviewer of contemporary Russian literature is obliged to dwell almost exclusively upon the monthly journals, as in consequence of the conditions of the book market, especially on account of the risk involved, the works of our con-temporary writers are rarely published in separate volumes.... If we come across a purely literary work published separately in book form, it generally belongs to the pen of a writer whose literary repu-tation stands very high and who consequently escapes all risk; or, on the contrary, it is the production of a beginner whose writings are ignored by the reviews, and who, being devoured by the passion-ate desire to see his work in type—in spite of his lack of talent— ventures everything to have it printed at any cost" (July 3, 26). The complaint that the editors of the Russian journals of that time would "publish nothing that risks disapproval," had been made earlier by Merezhkovsky in *On the Decline...* See Ralph Matlaw, "The Mani-festo of Russian Symbolism," *Slavic and East European Journal,* 15 (1957), 181.

28. Quoted in Ashukin, 105.

29. V. Khodasevich, *"Otryvki iz vospominanii," Sovremen-nye zapiski*, 23 (1925), 222.

30. Valerii Briusov, *"Detskie i iunosheskie vospominaniia," Novyi Mir* (December, 1926), 119.

31. *Dnevniki*, 28.

32. M. Gor'kii, *Sobranie sochinenii v tridtsati tomakh*, Vol. I, 383.

33. *Complete Works*, I, 152.

> *Iunosha blednyi so vzorom goriashchim,*
> *Nyne daiu ia tebe tri zaveta:*
> *Pervyi primi: ne zhivi nastoiashchim,*
> *Tol'ko griadushchee—oblast' poeta.*

Pomni vtoroi: nikomu ne sochuvstvui,
Sam zhe sebia poliubi bezpredel'no.
Tretii khrani: pokloniaisia iskusstvu,
Tol'ko emu, bezrazdumno, beztsel'no.

Iunosha blednyi so vzorom smushchennym!
Esli ty primesh' moikh tri zaveta,
Molcha padu ia boitsom pobezhdennym,
Znaia, chto v mire ostavliu poeta.

34. *Complete Works,* IV, 173. For a brilliant discussion of these two poems, see Erlich's *The Double Image.*

Ty dolzhen byt' gordym, kak znamia;
Ty dolzhen byt' ostrym, kak mech;
Kak Dantu, podzemnoe plamia
Dolzhno tebe shcheki obzhech'.

Vsego bud' kholodnyi svidetel',
Na vse ustremliaia svoi vzor,
Da budet tvoia dobrodetel'—
Gotovnost' vzoiti na koster.

Byt' mozhet vse v zhizni lish' sredstvo
Dlia iarko-pevuchikh stikhov,
I ty s bezpechal'nogo detstva
Ishchi sochetaniia slov.

V minuty liubovnykh ob''iatii
K bezstrast'iu sebia prinevol',
I v chas bezposhchadnykh raspiatii
Proslav' izstuplennuiu bol'.

V snakh utra i v bezdne vechernei
Lovi, chto shepnet tebe Rok,
I pomni: ot veka iz ternii
Poeta zavetnyi venok.

35. *Dnevniki,* 40-41.
36. *Dnevniki,* entry for April 9, 1898, 34.
37. *Ibid.,* entry for August 13, 1898, 47.

CHAPTER III

1. *"Avtobiografiia,"* 112.
2. *Dnevniki,* 52.
3. *Dnevniki,* 173 (note).
4. *Russkii arkhiv* (October), 618-31. In 1929 N. K. Piksanov published a bibliography of Briusov's publications on Pushkin containing eighty-two entries. Valerii Briusov, *Moi Pushkin,* ed. N. K. Piksanov (M. 1929), 309-17.

5. Rough draft of a letter to an unknown correspondent contained in Briusov's archives and quoted in Ashukin, 131-32.

6. G. I. Chulkov, "V. Ya. Briusov: vospominaniia 1900-1907 gg.," *Iskusstvo* (February, 1925), 243.

7. *Ibid.*

8. In reviewing Briusov's introduction, entitled *On Russian Versification (O russkom stikhoslozhenii), Monthly Works (Ezhemesiachnye sochineniia)* (August, 1900), called it "not bad" and said that it contained "several perceptive observations" (Bialik, *Russkaia literatura,* 458).

9. Introduction to the *Catalogue of Skorpion Publishing House* (M. 1902), probably written by Briusov. Quoted by Ashukin, 140.

10. "*Vospominaniia,*" 243-44.

11. "*Avtobiografiia,*" 114. Although according to Bunin, when Merezhkovsky first heard of "Skorpion" he exclaimed, "I'm tired, I'm not able any more! These intellectual masturbators, these grave diggers..." *(Dnevniki,* 91).

12. "*Avtobiografiia,*" 114. Yasinsky's praise *(Monthly Works)* [December, 1900]), was indeed enthusiastic: "Briusov is not only a poet but a thinker as well and is on the right road." But it is difficult to understand exactly why Briusov was so overjoyed with Gorky's review *(The Nizhgorod Page [Nizhegorodskii listok]* November, 14, 1900): "Although he now takes poetry more seriously, Briusov nevertheless still appears before the reader in strange and eccentric clothing, with an undefinable mood and with a clearly artificial disregard for the form and beauty of verse.... He dedicates poems to Alexander the Great and Casandra, he sings praises to Cleopatra, Orpheus, and many other deceased, in one poem he awakened Ramses.... It is difficult to read Briusov's poems, they are uneven, weighted with pretentiousness, and do not remain in one's memory." Gorky did, however, note several poems as more successful than others, namely "The Tale of a Robber" ("Skazanie o razboinike") and "To the New Bell" ("Na novyi kolokol") in which "the foundation of folk speech was excellently maintained." Both reviews quoted in Bialik, *Russkaia literatura,* 471-72.

13. "*Vospominaniia,*" 243.

14. *Dnevniki,* 91. In light of the review quoted above, either Briusov is exaggerating or Gorky was being polite.

15. Gorky declined the invitation to publish in *Northern Flowers* so as not to "irritate" his public by appearing in print with "rejected" Symbolists (Ashukin, 149-50). Unexpectedly, however, Chekhov agreed to publish his short story *At Night (Noch'iu)* in the almanac.

16. Andrei Belyi, *Nachalo veka* (M. 1933), 145.

17. "*Otryvki iz vospominanii,*" 217.

18. *Lug zelenyi* (M. 1910), 205.

19. "*Vospominaniia,*" 245.

20. The expression is Bely's, *Zapiski mechtatelei* (June, 1922). Quoted in Ashukin, 179.

21. Donchin, *The Influence of French Symbolism,* 40-41.

22. In February, 1902, Merezhkovsky asked Briusov point-blank if the latter believed in Christ. When Briusov answered that he did not,

Merezhkovsky was reduced to despair *(Dnevniki,* 115).

23. Georgii Chulkov, *Gody stranstvii* (M. 1930), 318.

24. Donchin, *The Influence of French Symbolism,* 42.

25. P. P. Pertsov, *"Briusov v nachale veka (Iz vospo-minanii),"* *Znamia* (March, 1940), 252.

26. *"Valerii Briusov i Novyi put',"* *Literaturnoe nasledstvo,* Vols. 27-28, 278.

27. Chulkov, *"Vospominaniia,"* 246.

28. Maksomov, *"Briusov i Novyi put',"* 278.

29. "We were given permission [to publish] *The Scales,* and this parted us for good with *The New Way" (Dnevniki,* 134, entry for October 26-31, 1903).

30. *"Avtobiografiia,"* 115.

31. Donchin, *The Influence of French Symbolism,* 161. Donchin presents an impressive argument that it was Briusov, and not Balmont, who was responsible for the introduction of the theme of the city into Russian Symbolist poetry. The influence on Briusov, in turn, came from Verhaeren.

32. November 25, 1903, quoted in Ashukin, 174.

33. Quoted in Ashukin, 174-76. P. P. Pertsov considers *Urbi et Orbi* Briusov's best collection, the one which "brought him out of his status as pupil and put him on a level with Balmont" *(Literaturnye vospominaniia,* 265).

34. P. 115. Further testimony to Briusov's intimate involvement with *The Scales* was neatly expressed by G. Chulkov: "For me the journal and the man merge into one" (quoted in Donchin, *The Influence of French Symbolism,* 45. According to Briusov's wife, "One may say with assurance that all unsigned articles in *The Scales* belong to Briusov; a series of signatures such as Avrely, V. Bakulin, Pentuar, Sbirko, Garmody, K. K. K., Ch., Tourist, A., R., Enrico., L., and others were Briusov's pseudonyms" *("Materialy,"* 135).

CHAPTER IV

1. See Donchin, *The Influence of French Symbolism,* 46-68.

2. See P. P. Pertsov: "1905 changed literature no less than 1895, although in a different sense: then it was marked by the birth of innovation, now by its changed aspect, and chiefly by its dissemination. After 1905 Symbolism is no longer derided and is quickly crowned with almost academic laurels" *(Literaturnye vospominaniia,* 266).

3. *Poeziia Valeriia Briusova,* 209.

4. Ashukin, 193-94.

5. Mochulsky, *Valerii Briusov,* 85.

6. Letter to P. P. Pertsov, January, 1905, quoted in P. P. Pertsov, *Literaturnye vospominaniia,* 265-66.

7. *"The Scales:* The Story of a Russian Magazine," *Slavic and East European Journal* 38 (1958), 222-23.

8. *Russian Symbolism: A Study of Vyacheslav Ivanov and the Russian Symbolist Esthetic* (London, 1970), 2-3.

9. *Pis'ma A. Bloka k rodnym,* letter from March 28, 1905. Quoted in Ashukin, 194.

10. "Russian Poets in Search of a Poetics," *Comparative Literature* 4 (1952), 55.

11. See, for example, Bely's characteristic report: "And later... we would argue about a great deal; about the meaning of French Symbolism, not too significant for Blok and me and significant for Briusov." *Na rubezhe dvukh stoletii*, 7.

12. Quoted in Erlich, *ibid*.

13. *"K istorii simvolizma,"* reprinted in K. Loks, *"Briusov-teoretik simvolizma," Literaturnoe nasledstvo*, Vols., 27-28, 270. Subsequent references to pages of this article will be given in the text.

14. Moscow: *Tovarishchestvo tipografii A. I. Mamontova.* As to why Briusov titled his book *On Art* instead of the expected *About Art* is remarked upon in his *"Avtobiografiia"* where he writes: "None other than L. I. Polivanov assured me that the preposition *'ob'* was placed only *before pronouns"* (110). The inspiration for *On Art* dates from the year of its publication when Briusov wrote the following letter to Leo Tolstoy upon the appearance of the latter's *What is Art? (Chto takoe iskusstvo?):* "Count Lev Niko-laevich! I was only recently able to become familiar with your article on art since I was in bed ill all through Christmas. I was not surprised that you did not mention my name in the long list of your predecessors, because undoubtedly you did not know my views on art. However, it is precisely I who should occupy the first place on your list because my views coincide almost literally with yours. I explained these views of mine—still not completely thought out— in the introduction to the first edition of my little book *Chefs d'Oeuvre* which appeared in 1895. I am attaching hereunto that introduction. You will see that I was standing upon that road which would have led me to the very same conclusions at which you arrived. I would not like that fact to remain unknown to the readers of your article. And you, of course, would not want to take from me, similar to the rich man in Nathan's parable, my "only lamb." It will be easy for you to correct your inadvertent error by making a note in the second half of your article or in its separate issue, or, finally, by a special letter to the newspapers. Most respectfully yours, Valery Briusov. P. S. I never would have allowed myself to address you by letter, but my illness will probably prevent me from going outdoors for several weeks" (quoted in Ashukin, 116-17).

15. *On Art,* 12. Subsequent references to pages in this book will be given in the text.

16. "In poetry, in art, the artist's personality itself is primary! It *is* the essence, everything else is form! ... any enjoyment of art is communication with the artist's soul.... Here is the true unity of people, unattainable to them by any other means; [this unity] is the true aim of art!" Letter to Pertsov, March 14, 1895. *Pis'ma V. Ya. Briusova k P. P. Pertsovu: 1894-1896 gg.* (M. 1927), 13.

17. Again Briusov expressed a similar thought three years earlier in a letter to Pertsov (April 1, 1895): "...a Symbolist must be more afraid of banality than of anything else." Pertsov, *Pis'ma*, 18. The next time Briusov attacked "art for art's sake" was in 1904 in his "manifesto," *"Kliuchi tain,"* printed in *The Scales* (Vol. 1, no. 1): "[Art for art's sake] divorces art from life, that is, from the only ground upon which anything may grow in mankind. Art in the name

of aimless beauty (with a large B) is dead art" (13). This is an interesting echo of Baudelaire, whose works Briusov of course knew well: "The childish utopianism of the school of art for art's sake... was doomed to sterility. Art for art's sake was a flagrant defiance of human nature." *L'Art Romantic,* in *Oeuvres Completes de Charles Baudelaire,* 19 vols., ed. Jacques Crepet (Paris, 1925), III, 296.

18. Letter from August 17, 1895. Pertsov, *Pis'ma,* 36.

19. *Ibid.,* 36-37.

20. In many respects Andrei Bely shared several views with Briusov relating to inspiration and craft. Bely has also expressed views close to those of Briusov concerning the sources of a work of art: "In so far as a symbol is an image that is carried into life by experience, the Symbolists point to the triple source of a symbol; every symbol is a triad, 'abc,' where 'a' is the indivisible creative unity in which are combined two items ('b' the image of nature, embodied in sound, color, and word, and 'c' experience, which freely makes available the material of sounds, color, and word so that this material wholly expresses the experience); here is freedom (not tyranny) and subordination only to that creative norm, which, not being given from without by any laws, realizes its goals; sometimes art is directed to be ideological, to express some tendency or other, or, the reverse: not to express any tendencies. Both the 'art for art's sake tendency as well as the 'art as a means of parochial struggle' tendency are equally as hampering to the Symbolist artist. And that is why the representatives [of both these tendencies] met the profession of Symbolism so adversely." Written in 1909 and published in *"Na perevale,"* Arabeski (M. 1911), 245.

21. Letter to P. P. Pertsov, dated April 17, 1895, in Pertsov, *Pis'ma,* 20.

22. *"Briusov-kritik,"* in *Istoriia russkoi kritiki,* 2 vols., ed. B. P. Gorodetskii *et al.* (M. 1968), II, 630.

23. Among many testimonials to Briusov's importance as a teacher the following words of Bely are typical: "I have considered, I do consider, and I will consider Briusov my closest teacher after V. Solovyov," letter to G. Chulkov, August 26, 1907. Quoted in Ashukin, 224. Kornei Chukovsky also paid tribute to Briusov as a teacher: Briusov pulled me out of the newspaper quagmire.... He got me used to great literature and directed me in my first years of work. He never once during this time assumed the pose of a teacher. The whole strength and charm of his pedagogy was precisely in the fact that his pedagogy was unnoticeable." K. Chukovsky *Repin, Gor'kii, Briusov: vospominaniia* (M. 1940), 176.

24. Briusov expressed himself again on this subject in 1906, in an article published in *The Golden Fleece (Zolotoe runo):* "I think... that true art was always realistic. Poets never knew any other task except the reproduction of life's truth... It was only the notion itself of truth that changed.... The Decadents knew no other truth than the truth of the moment and stamped into their poetry the moments of life in all their vagueness.... But upon all banners of art there has always stood one and the same motto: Truth" *"Karl V (Dialog o realizme v iskusstve),"*(April), 66.

25. *"Sviashchennaia zhertva,"* 29. Subsequent page numbers from this article will be given in the text.

26. Quoted in *"Sviashchennaia zhertva,"* 23. Whether Briusov was quoting these lines from memory when he wrote his article is not clear; however, in Pushkin's *Polnoe sobranie sochinenii,* 16 vols. in 20 (Moscow, 1937-1949) instead of *v zaboty, v zabotakh* is given and instead of *vnushaet, vkushaet* is given. There are no variants indicated.

> *Poka ne trebuet poeta*
> *K sviashchennoi zhertve Apollon,*
> *V zaboty* (sic) *suetnogo sveta*
> *On malodushno pogruzhen.*
> *Molchit ego sviataia lira,*
> *Dusha vnushaet* (sic) *khladnyi son,*
> *I mezh detei nichtozhnykh mira,*
> *Byt' mozhet, vsekh nichtozhnei on.*

27. *Complete Works,* IV, 173.

> *Byt' mozhet, vse v zhizni lish' sredstvo*
> *Dlia iarko-pevuchikh stikhov.*

28. *The Double Image,* 77.

29. *Gedenkausgabe der Werke, Briefe und Gespräche,* 2nd ed., 27 vols., ed. Ernst Beutler (Zurich, Stuttgart, 1961-1971), I, 167.

> When she succumbs to sleep, pondering, long I lie still.
> Often too in her arms I've lain composing a poem,
> Gently with fingering hand count the hexameter's beat
> Out on her back.

The English translation is by Michael Hamburger in Stephen Spender, ed., *Great Writings of Goethe* (New York, 1958), 228-29.

30. *Selected Essays: 1917-1932* (London, 1932), 21.

31. New York, 1931.

32. "On Literary Technique," in *The Art of Poetry,* trans. by D. Folliot (New York, 1958), 315-37.

33. Quoted in Noel Stock, *The Life of Ezra Pound* (New York, 1970), 88.

34. *The Scales* (May, 1905), 38.

35. *Sobranie sochinenii,* 6 vols. (M. 1965-1969), VI, 58.

36. *"Sviashchennaia zhertva,"* 26.

37. René Wellek and Austin Warren, *Theory of Literature,* 3rd ed. (New York, 1956), 84.

38. *The Art of Poetry,* xiii.

39. Quoted in Georgii Chulkov, *Vospominaniia,"* 249.

> *Vpered, mechta, moi vernyi vol!*
> *Nevolei, esli ne okhotoi.*
> *Ia bliz tebia, moi knut tiazhel,*
> *Ia sam truzhus', i ty rabotai.*

40. *The Life of Ezra Pound,* 12. Although it is beyond the scope of this work, a study of Briusov and Pound would make a valuable contribution to the problem of creative genius of a specific kind. Both were "makers" rather than "possessed" or "seers." Aspects of their respective careers show an amazing similarity. Both sought intensely after personal glory, both were outstanding translators, both were journalists, both founded a literary school (and both were subsequently disowned by the school), both were men of almost unlimited erudition, both were intensely disliked by many of their contemporaries but respected for their abilities, and, perhaps most significant, both were teachers of poets greater than they—Pound of Eliot and Joyce, Briusov of Bely and Blok. Even in their personal eccentricities they evidence striking parallels; for example, both were interested in the occult and were notorious as anti-Semites.

41. *Dalekie i blizkie,* 117-18.

CHAPTER V

1. *"Avtobiografiia,"* 115.

2. See Bely's remarks in *"Lirika i eksperiment":* "Briusov's iambic tetrameter from the period of *Stephanos* is quite clearly connected with the rhythm of Pushkin's Lyceum poems.... The period when Briusov was working on Pushkin's [poems] corresponds approximately with the period of *Stephanos'* creation." *Simvolizm* (M. 1910), 276. In the same passage Bely remarks on the similarity of Briusov's verses to those of Zhukovsky as well.

3. Maksimov, *Poeziia Valeriia Briusova,* 217.

4. By 1907, however, Bely, Blok, and others were also publishing in these journals.

5. *"Avtobiografiia,"* 115.

6. *"Valerii Yakovlevich Briusov," Sovremennye zapiski* 22 (1924), 422.

7. *"Vospominaniia,"* 246.

8. Letter to V. S. Miroliubov, August 19, 1905. L. N. Andreev, "Letters to V. S. Miroliubov (1899-1907)," *Literaturnyi arkhiv,* Vol. V (M. 1960), 178.

9. Chulkov, *Gody stranstvii,* 227. In a letter written to Chulkov sometime between November 1 and December 31, 1905, Briusov still insisted "I will not participate [in *The Scales'*] editorial affairs," *ibid.,* 340. Briusov's intention to cease participating actively in *The Scales'* affairs is also attested to by Bely in a letter to Blok written in September, 1905: "Do not forget *The Scales.* Please send something. *The Scales* needs help now. V[alery] Ya[kovlevich] does not want to participate actively, for he has been carrying out *everything* alone." A. A. Blok-Andrei Belyi, *Perepiska* (M. 1940), 139.

10. Quoted in Ashukin, 208.

11. *"Aleksandr Blok i Andrei Belyi v 1907 godu," Literaturnoe nasledstvo,* Vols. 27-28, 372.

12. Actually the variety of philosophies and factions vying for precedence in Russian literary circles at this time was far greater than this small listing indicates. Others will be mentioned below.

13. Viacheslav Ivanov, *"Kop'e Afiny," The Scales* (October,

1904), 13-14.

14. *Ibid.*, 14.

15. See *"Nitsshe i Dionis," The Scales* (May, 1904), 17-30.

16. *Ibid.*, 22, 26.

17. *The Scales* (March), 1-8.

18. *Sobranie sochinenii,* Vol. V: *Proza 1903-1917,* ed. V. N. Orlov *et al.* (M. 1962), 426. Subsequent references to pages in this article will be given in the text.

19. *The Scales* (September), 53-57. The article is signed with the pseudonym V. Bakulin.

20. *"Torzhestvo pobeditelei,"* 55, italics in the original. Page reference to this article will be given in the text.

21. *Nachalo veka,* 160. Bely is making a play on words when he uses the term "mother country" which can also be translated as "center (of empire)." The Russian for this term is *metropoliia* and the editorial offices of *The Scales* were located in the *Metropole* [*Metropol'*] hotel in Moscow.

22. Maksimov, *Poeziia Valeriia Briusova,* 217.

23. Letter in Bely's archive quoted by Maksimov, *ibid.*

24. For a detailed account of Bely's relations with Briusov see Oleg Maslenikov, *The Frenzied Poets* (Berkeley, 1952), 99-127.

25. *Nachalo veka,* 413-14.

26. *"Simvolizm i sovremennoe russkoe iskusstvo,"* 38. Subsequent page references to this article will be given in the text.

27. *"O podpiske na 'Vesy' 1909 g. Ot redaktsii i kontory"* (November), 89.

28. Although in fairness to Briusov, it should be pointed out that Chulkov wrote that Briusov was the only one of those who attacked him with whom he bothered to carry on polemics, for all the others were motivated by ulterior, non-literary reasons. *Gody stranstvii,* 248.

29. *The Frenzied Poets,* 120.

30. Bely, *Nachalo veka,* 386 and *The Frenzied Poets,* 119.

31. *The Frenzied Poets,* 119.

32. Above it was stated that *The Scales* in its early years expressed the essence of French Symbolism and that Briusov's understanding of Symbolism was close, if not identical, to that of the French. In this light it seems even more natural that Briusov take over criticism in the journal's management. See Donchin: "If one supports the generally accepted interpretation of French Symbolism, namely that the Symbolist school created a revolution not so much in poetry itself as in ideas about poetry—*The Scales* offers an excellent example by its preponderant attention to critical works" *(67).*

33. For an account of Briusov's popularity at this time, see D. Maksimov, *Poeziia Valeriia Briusova,* 204-06.

34. *Nachalo veka,* 386.

35. "Russian Poets in Search of a Poetics," 57-58.

36. *Na rubezhe dvukh stoletii,* 198.

37. *Ibid.*, 198-200.

38. *Lug zelenyi* (New York, 1967), 199.

39. December, 1909, 185-91.

40. *Na rubezhe dvukh stoletii,* 195.

41. *Apollon* (September, 1910), 33.

42. *Ibid.* See Maksimov: "[Briusov's] argument against the 'Mystics' rested upon his doctrine of 'free art.' This causes us to consider the essential foundation of the Briusovian anti-mysticism to be his traditional individualism and his attempts at independence from any kind of 'extra-subjective,' 'absolute' norms.... The sobriety and clarity of Briusov's world view was in itself sufficient defense against mystical interest" *(Poeziia Valeriia Briusova,* 219-20).

43. "Yeats," in *On Poetry and Poets* (New York, 1961), 299.

44. "The poetic generation born after 1885 contined the revolutionary and cultural work of the Symbolists—but ceased to be Symbolists... About 1910 the Symbolist school began to disintegrate...." D. S. Mirsky, *A History of Russian Literature* (New York, 1949), 485. There are other historians of the period, however, who feel that 1910 marks only a change in the movement's nature. Pertsov, for example, says that in this year "the era of *early Symbolism* began to end." *Literaturnye vospominaniia,* 267 (my italics). In Bely's phrase, "a swing of the axis took place." *Nachalo veka,* 375.

45. *The Frenzied Poets,* 222.

46. Quoted in Ashukin, 264.

47. G. Lelevich, *"Desiat' pisem Valeriia Briusova k P. P. Pertsovu," Pechat' i revoliutsiia* (July, 1926), 46.

48. *"Debiutanty," The Scales* (March, 1908), 77-78.

49. *Ibid.,* 78.

50. Not only does this support the view stated above that Briusov's poetry had much in common with the Acmeists, it also supports D. Chizhevskij's following observation: "It is thoroughly possible too that in a more distant perspective of the future all the modernistic 'unrealistic' movements in Russian literature between 1895-1925 will be conceived of as one great—though differentiated—unity." *Comparative History of Slavic Literatures,* ed. S. A. Zenkovsky and trans. R. N. Porter and M. P. Rice (Nashville, 1971), 197.

51. *On Poetry and Poets,* 297.

52. See, for example, Mirsky's comments on this period of Briusov's creative work: "Beginning with *Vse napevy,* Briusov begins to become his own epigon and begins to decline. ....Briusov began to move away from Symbolism, he tried to lower his style. In place of his solemn and tense eroticism there appeared some kind of deliberate nihilism of passion.... He did not lose the power of the craftsman, but his verse became unnecessary, dead." *"Valerii Yakovlevich Briusov,"* 423.

53. Ashukin, 355.

CONCLUSION

1. Ernst Cassirer, *An Essay on Man* (New York, 1970), 18.

2. *Sobranie sochinenii,* Vol. IV, ed. G. P. Struve and B. A. Fillipov (Washington, 1968), 287-88.

3. *Selected Essays* (London, 1932), 17.

4. Moscow, 1918, 42, my italics.

5. *Dalekie i blizkie,* 115-16.

6. *"Valerii Yakovlevich Briusov,"* 418.

BIBLIOGRAPHY

The most complete bibliography of Briusov's work published to date is that of T. J. Binyon, "Bibliography of the works of Valery Briusov," OXFORD SLAVONIC PAPERS, XII (1956), 117-140. It includes the many hundreds of separate poems, stories, dramatic works, translations, letters, reviews, and miscellaneous items that are scattered throughout dozens of Russian and Soviet journals, books, and newspapers.

Aikhenval's, Yu. I. "Valerii Briusov." SILUETY RUSSKIKH PISATELEI. M. 1910.

Anichkov, E. "Poslednie pobedy russkoi poezii." ZOLOTOE RUNO, no. 2; nos. 3-4 (1908), 45-55; 103-112.

———. NOVAIA RUSSKAIA POEZIIA. Slavistic Printings and Reprintings, Vol. CLXXX-VII. The Hague, 1969.

Ashukin, N. "Briusov i knigi." KNIGA I PROLETARSKAIA REVOLIUTSIIA (October, 1939), 182-184.

———. "Trud V. Briusova." NOVYI MIR (October, 1934), 230-238.

———. VALERII BRIUSOV V AVTOBIOGRAFICHESKIKH ZAPISIAKH, PIS'MAKH VOSPOMINANIIAKH SOVREMENNIKOV I OTZYVAKH KRITIKI. M., 1929.

Batiushkova, F. D. "Valerii Briusov. ISTORIIA RUSSKOI LITERATURY XX VEKA. Vol. I. Edited by S. A. Vengerov. M., 1914, pp. 119-134.

Belyi, Andrei. ARABESKI. Slavische Propyläen, Vol. LXIII. Munich, 1969.

———. LUG ZELENYI. The Slavic Series, Vol. V. New York, 1967.

———. MEZHDU DVUKH REVOLIUTSII. Russian Study Series, Vol. LX. Chicago, 1966.

———. NA RUBEZHE DVUKH STOLETII. Rarity Reprints. Vol. IV. Chicago, 1966.

———. NACHALO VEKA. Russian Study Series, Vol. LXI. Chicago, 1966.

———. "Poeziia Valeriia Briusova." NOVYI PUT' (July, 1904), 133-139.

———. SIMVOLIZM. Slavische Propyläen, Vol. LXII. Munich, 1969.

———. VOSPOMINANIIA O A. A. BLOKE. Slavische Propyläen, Vol. XLVII. Munich, 1969.

Bialik, B. A., ed. RUSSKAIA LITERATURA KONTSA XIX-NACHALA XX VEKA. DE-VIANOSTYE GODY. M., 1968.

Blagoi, D. D. "Valerii Briusov." TRI VEKA' IZ ISTORII RUSSKOI POEZII XVIII, XIX I XX VV' M., 1933, pp. 341-63.

Blok, Aleksandr. "O sovremennom sostoianii russkogo simvolizma." SOBRANIE SOCHI-NENII. Vol. V. Edited by V. N. Orlov. M., 1962, pp. 425-436.

———. ZAPISNYE KNIZHKI. 1901-1920. Edited by V. N. Orlov, A. A. Surkov, and K. I. Chukovskii. M., 1965.

———, and Belyi, Andrei. PEREPISKA. Slavische Propyläen, Vol. LXV. Munich, 1969.

Briusov, Valerii. "Pis'ma k P. P. Pertsovu." RUSSKII SOVREMENNIK (April, 1924), 227-235.

Briusova, I. "Materialy k biografii Valeriia Briusova." V. Briusov. IZBRANNYE STIKHI. M., 1933, pp. 119-149.

Cherepakhov, Matvei Samoilovich. RUSSKAIA PERIODICHESKAIA PECHAT' (1895-OKTIABR' 1917). M., 1957.

Chernov, Victor. "Eros i mechta v poezii Valeriia Briusova." ZAVETY (December, 1913), 51-74.

Chikhachev, P. "Moskovskie vstrechi." DON (March, 1958), 157-164.

Chistova, I. S. "Pis'ma V. Ya. Briusova k A. F. Oneginu. (K istorii pushkinovedcheskikh issledovanii Briusova)." FILOLOGICHESKIE NAUKI 14 (1971), 84-91.

Chukovskii, Kornei. REPIN; GOR'KII, MAIAKOVSKII, BRIUSOV. VOSPOMINANIIA. M., 1940.

Chulkov, Georgii. POKRYVALO IZIDY: KRITICHESKIE OCHERKI. M., 1909.

———. "V. Ya. Briusov. Vospominaniia 1900-1907 gg." ISKUSSTVO (February, 1925), 241-256.

———. "Vesy." APOLLON (July, 1910), 15-20.

Cizevskij, Dmitrij. COMPARATIVE HISTORY OF SLAVIC LITERATURES. Translated by Richard Noel Porter and Martin P. Rice. Edited by Serge A. Zenkovsky. Nashville, 1971.

Donchin, Georgette. THE INFLUENCE OF FRENCH SYMBOLISM ON RUSSIAN POETRY. Slavistic Printings and Reprintings, Vol. XIX. The Hague, 1958.

Eliot, T. S. SELECTED ESSAYS: 1917-1932. London, 1932.

———. "Introduction" to Valéry, Paul. THE ART OF POETRY. Translated by D. Folliot. New York, 1958.

———. ON POETRY AND POETS' New York, 1969.

Erlich, Victor. "Images of the Poet and of Poetry in Slavic Romanticism and Neo-Romanticism (Krasinki, Brjusov, Blok)." AMERICAN CONTRIBUTION TO THE FIFTH INTERNATIONAL CONGRESS OF SLAVISTS, SOFIA, SEPTEMBER 1963. Vol. II: LITERARY CONTRIBUTIONS. Slavistic Printings and Reprintings, Vol. X. The Hague, 1963.

———. "Russian Poets in Search of a Poetics." COMPARATIVE LITERATURE (April, 1952), 54-74.

———. THE DOUBLE IMAGE: CONCEPTS OF THE POET IN SLAVIC LITERATURES. Baltimore, 1964.

Fowlie, Wallace. MALLARME. Chicago, 1962.

Giliarovskii, V. MOSKVA I MOSKVICHI. Rostov-na-Donu, 1958, pp. 378-82.

Gindin, S. "Neosushchestvlennyi zamysel Briusova." VOPROSY LITERATURY 14 (1970), 189-203.

Goethe, Johann Wolfgang von. GEDENKSAUSGABE DER WERKE, BRIEFE UND GESPRÄCHE. Vol. I. 2nd ed. Edited by Ernst Beutler. Zurich, 1961.

Gofman, Modest. KNIGA O RUSSKIKH POETAKH POSLEDNEGO DESIATILETIIA. OCHERKI, STIKHOTVORENIIA, AVTOGRAFY. St. Petersburg, 1909.

Gol'tsev, V. V. "Briusov i Blok (po neopublikovannym materialam)." PECHAT' I REVOLIUTSIIA (April, May, 1928), 33-46; 67-80.

———. STAT'I I OCHERKI. M., 1958, pp. 71-78.

Gornitskaia, N. S. "Briusov—kritik." ISTORIIA RUSSKOI KRITIKI. Vol. II. Edited by B. P. Gorodetskii. M., 1958, pp. 629-645.

Gorodetskii, Sergei. " Valerii Briusov (K godovshchine smerti 1924 g.—9 oktiabria 1925 g.)." KRASNAIA NIVA, no. 41 (1925), 979.

Grigor'ev, M. "Valerii Briusov v poslednie gody zhizni." PROZHEKTOR (March, 1925), 19-22.

Grigor'ian, K. N. "Verlaine and Russian Symbolism." SOVIET STUDIES IN LITERATURE 7, iv (Fall, 1971), 313-335.

Grossman, L. P. BOR'BA ZA STIL'. M., 1927.

———. "Briusov i frantsuzskie simvolisty." OT PUSHKINA DO BLOKA. M., 1926, pp. 331-341.

Gudzii, N. "Yunosheskoe tvorchestvo Briusova." LITERATURNOE NASLEDSTVO. Vols. 27-28. M, 1937.

Gumilev, N. SOBRANIE SOCHINENII V CHETYREKH TOMAKH. Vol. IV. Edited by G. P. Struve and B. A. Filippov. Washington, 1968.

Gurevich, L. "Nemetskii romantizm i simvolizm nashego vremeni." RUSSKAIA MYSL' (April, 1914), 102-110.

Holthusen, Johannes. STUDIEN ZUR AESTHETIK UND POETIK DES RUSSISCHEN SYMBOLISMUS. Göttingen, 1957.

———. TWENTIETH-CENTURY RUSSIAN LITERATURE: A CRITICAL STUDY Translated by Theodore Huebner. New York, 1972.

Khodasevich, Vladislav. LITERATURNYE STAT'I I VOSPOMINANIIA. New York, 1954.

———. "Otryvki iz vospominanii." SOVREMENNYE ZAPISKI, 23 (1925), 212-236.

Kogan, P. S. "Literaturnye napravleniia i kritika 80-kh i 90-kh godov." ISTORIIA RUSS-
KOI LITERATURY XIX VEKA. Vol. V. Edited by D. N. Ovsiano-Kulikovskii.
M., 1911.
———. "Pamiati Briusova." MOLODAIA GVARDIIA (September, 1924), 168-72.
———. ed. VALERIU BRIUSOVU. SBORNIK, POSVIASHCHENNYI 50-TILETIIU SO
DNIA ROZHDENIIA POETA. M., 1924.
Lelevich, G. "Desiat' pisem Valeriia Briusova k P. P. Pertsovu." PECHAT' I REVOLIU-
TSIIA (July, 1926), 36-50.
LITERATURNYE MANIFESTY OT SIMVOLIZMA K OKTIABRIU. Edited by N. L.
Brodskii, V. L'vov Rogachevskii, and N. P. Sidorov. Slavistic Printings and Reprint-
ings, Vol. CXXXV. The Hague, 1969.
Loks, K. "Briusov—teoretik simvolizma." LITERATURNOE NASLEDSTVO. Vols. 27-
28. M, 1937.
Lunacharskii, A. V. "Briusov i revoliutsiia." PECHAT' I REVOLIUTSIIA (June, 1924),
1-13.
———. LITERATURNYE SILUETY. M., 1925.
Magurie, Robert A. "Macrocosm or Microcosm? The Symbolists on Russia." REVIEW OF
NATIONAL LITERATURES, 3, i (Spring, 1972), 125-152.
Makovskii, F. "Chto takoe russkoe dekadenstvo?" OBRAZOVANIE (September, 1905),
125-142.
Maksimov, D. BRIUSOV: POEZIIA I POZITSIIA. L., 1969.
———. "Poeticheskoe tvorchestvo Valeriia Briusova." V. Briusov. STIKHOTVORE-
NIIA I POEMY. Edited by M. I. Dikman. L, 1961.
———. POEZIIA VALERIIA BRIUSOVA. L, 1940.
———. "Valerii Briusov i NOVYI PUT'." LITERATURNOE NASLEDSTVO. Vols. 27-28.
M., 1937.
Maslenikov, Oleg. A. THE FRENZIED POETS: ANDREY BIELY AND THE RUSSIAN
SYMBOLISTS. Berkeley, 1952.
Medvedskii, K. "Simvolizm na russkoi pochve." NABLIUDATEL' (janury, 1894), 314-
333.
Meilakh, B. "Simvolisty v 1905 godu." LITERATURNOE NASLEDSTVO. Vols. 27-28.
M., 1937.
Mirskii, D. S. "Valerii Yakovlevich Briusov." SOVREMENNYE ZAPISKI, 22 (1924),
414-426.
——[Mirsky]. A HISTORY OF RUSSIAN LITERATURE. Edited and abridged by Fran-
cis J. Whitfield. New York, 1949.
Mikhailovskii, B. V. "V. Ya. Briusov." ISTORIIA RUSSKOI SOVETSKOI LITERATURY,
Vol. I. 2nd ed. Edited by A. G. Demen'tev. M., 1967.
Mochul'skii, K. B. VALERII BRIUSOV. Paris, 1962.
Mohrenschildt, D. S. von. "The Russian Symbolist Movement." PMLA. 53 (1938), 1193-
1209.
Muratova, K. D., ed. LITERATURNYI ARKHIV. Vol. V. M, 1960.
Nevedomskii, M. "V zashchitu khudozhestva. (O nashikh 'modernistakh,' 'mistikakh,'
'mifotvortsakh' i t. d.)." SOVREMENNYI MIR (March and April, 1908), 211-229;
204-243.
Nikolaev, N. N. "Russkie simvolisty i koe-chto o simvolizme voobshche." RUSSKOE
OBOZRENIE (September, 1895), 362-372.
Novikov, Ivan. "Velikii truzhenik (Valerii Briusov)." POVESTI I RASSKAZY. M., 1958,
pp. 606-609.
Pertsov, P. P. "Briusov v nachale veka." ZNAMIA (March, 1940), 247-256.
———. LITERATURNYE VOSPOMINANIIA: 1890-1902 GG. M., 1933.
———. PIS'MA V. YA. BRIUSOVA K P. P. PERTSOVU (1894-1896 GG.). Teksty i mater-
ialy, Vol. III. M., 1927.
Poggioli, Renato. THE POETS OF RUSSIA:1890-1930. Cambridge, 1960.

Pogorelova, V. "Valerii Briusov i ego okruzhenie." NOVYI ZHURNAL, 33(1953), 176-198.

Pokrovskii, A. I. "Sovremennoe dekadenstvo pered sudom vekovechnykh idealov." RUSS-KII VESTNIK (June, 1904), 543-594.

Polianin, A. "Po povodu poslednikh proizvedenii V. Briusova." SEVERNYE ZAPISKI (January, 1917). 157-162.

Polonskii, V. "Pis'ma Maksima Gor'kogo k Valeriiu Briusovu." PECHAT' I REVOLIU-TSIIA (May, 1928), 54-66.

Postupal'skii, Igor'. "Poeziia Valeriia Briusova." V. Briusov. IZBRANNYE STIKHI. Edited by I. Postupal'skii. M., 1933.

———. "Proza Valeriia Briusova. V. Briusov. NEIZDANNAIA PROZA. Edited by I. M. Briusova. M., 1934. M., 1934.

Reeve, F. D. "Dobroliubov and Briusov: Symbolist Extremists." SLAVIC AND EAST EUROPEAN JOURNAL, 8 (1964), 191-301.

———. "VESY: A Study of a Russian Magazine." SLAVIC AND EAST EUROPEAN JOURNAL, 37 (1958), 221-235.

Rozanov, V. V. "O simvolistakh." RUSSKOE OBOZRENIE (September, 1896), 318—34.

Schmidt, Alexander. VALERIJ BRJUSOVS BEITRAG ZUR LITERATURTHEORIE. AUS DER GESCHICHTE DES RUSSISHCEN SYMBOLISMUS. Slavistische Beiträge, Vol. VII. Munich, 1963.

Skabichevskii, A. M. "Novye techeniia v sovremennoi literature." RUSSKAIA MYSL' (November, 1901), 81-100.

Solov'ev, V. S. "Russkie simvolisty." VESTNIK EVROPY (August, 1894; January and October, 1895), 890-892; 421-424; 847-851.

Stepanov, N. "Pushkin v izuchenii V. Ya. Briusova." KNIZHNYE NOVOSTI (June, 1937), 53-56.

Struk, Danylo. "The Great Escape: Principal Themes in Valerij Brjusov's Poetry." SLAVIC AND EAST EUROPEAN JOURNAL, 12 (1968), 407-423.

Stock, Noel. THE LIFE OF EZRA POUND. New York, 1970.

Symons, Arthur. THE SYMBOLIST MOVEMENT IN LITERATURE. New York, 1958.

Tschöpl, Carin. VJACESLAV IVANOV: DICHTUNG UND DICHTUNGSTHEORIE. Slavistische Beiträge, Vol. XXX. Munich, 1968.

Tsvetaeva, M. PROZA. New York, 1953.

Tynianov, Yurii N. ARKHAISTY I NOVATORY. Slavische Propyläen, Vol. XXXI. Munich, 1967.

Vengerov, S. A., ed. RUSSKAIA LITERATURA XX VEKA. 3 vols. M., 1914-1918.

Vengerova, Z. "Poety-simvolisty v Frantsii." VESTNIK EVROPY (September, 1892), 115-143.

Vidnes, Mariia. "Vladimir Solov'ev i simvolisty." SCANDO-SLAVICA, 13 (1967), 67-76.

Vipper, S. "Simvolizm v chelovecheskoi mysli i tvorchestve." RUSSKAIA MYSL. (February, 1905), 98-116.

Vnuchkov, V. "Dva pis'ma V. Ya. Briusova." MOSKVA, 13, xi (1969), 193-195.

West, James. RUSSIAN SYMBOLISM: A STUDY OF VYACHESLAV IVANOV AND THE RUSSIAN SYMBOLIST AESTHETIC. London, 1970.

Wilson, Edmund. AXEL'S CASTLE: A STUDY IN THE IMAGINATIVE LITERATURE OF 1870-1930. New York, 1959.

Yablonskii, S. "V. Ya. Briusov." VOZROZHDENIE, 13 (1950), 85-90.

Zhirmunskii, V. VALERII BRIUSOV I NASLEDIE PUSHKINA. Peterburg, 1922.

INDEX

Laforgue, 27, 28, 70
Lang, A. A. (A. Miropolsky), 31, 33, 39
Lebedev, 52
Lermontov, Yu., M., 12, 26, 111, 122
Leskov, 26
Lessing, 21
Les Trésors (Maeterlinck), 46
Liatsky, E. A., 90
Likiardopulo, 109
Listopad. See Falling of the Leaves, The
Literary craftsmanship. See Briusov, Valery Yakovlevich: esthetic views; Eliot, T. S.; Pound,
     Ezra; Valéry, Paul
LITO (Literary Division of Narkompros), 120
Liubov Alekseevna (governess), 14
Lokhvitskaia, Mirra, 7
Lug zelenyi. See Green Meadow, The
Maeterlinck, 27, 46, 50, 105
Makovsky, 117
Maksimov, D. (critic), 62, 66, 132 n
Mallarmé, 27, 28, 31, 37, 70-71
Mandelshtam, 46
Marryat, 12
Maslenikov, Oleg (critic), 108-109, 115
Marx, 105
Marxists, 105
Mayne-Reid, 12, 17
Medvedkovo, 13
"Meonism," 105
Merezhkovsky, D., 5, 6, 7, 26, 27, 28, 29, 38, 51-52, 53, 56, 58, 60-62, 66-67, 70, 74,
     91, 105, 117, 122, 134-135 n
Messenger of Europe, The (Vestnik Evropy), 27, 31, 35
Mikhailovsky, 3, 5, 6, 34, 39
Minsky, N. M. (pseudonym for N. M. Vilenkin), 4, 5, 6, 7, 38, 51, 105, 117
Mir Bozhii. See God's World
Miroliubov, V. S. (publisher), 91, 92
Mirsky, D. S., 90, 91, 127
Mochulsky, K. (critic), 128-129 n
Modernism, 66, 67, 68, 118, 141 n; beginnings, 3-7; Briusov's impact on, 125-127;
     definition of, 67; difference between and Symbolism, 104-105, 122; groups
     comprising, according to Bely, 105
Mohammed, 105
Moréas, 27, 28
Morozov, Nikolai A., 9
Morozova, V. A., 58
Moscow: differences between Moscow Symbolists and St. Petersburg Symbolists, 37,
     61-62, 65, 68, 74, 118, 131 n
"Musaget" (publishing house), 117
Mystical Anarchists, 101, 102, 105, 108, 110, 113
"Mystics." See "Clarists and Mystics"
Myth. See Ivanov, Viacheslav: philosophy of art

Nabliudatel'. See Observer, The
Nachalo veka. See Beginning of the Century, The

Poe, Edgar Allan, 39
Poet and the Crowd, The (Poet i tolpa) (Pushkin), 95-97
"Poet and the Mob, The" ("Poet i chern") (V. Ivanov), 95-97
"Poet, The" (Pushkin), 79, 83
Poètes maudits (Verlaine), 29
Poggioli, Renato, 40, 131 n
Poliakov, S. A., 55-56, 64, 108-109
Polivanov, L. I., 21; Polivanov's Gymnasium, 21-22, 23, 26-27, 129 n, 130 n
Polonsky, 5, 12
Polycrates, 53
Pound, Ezra, 81, 82, 83-84, 87, 88; similarities to Briusov, 139 n
Pre-Raphaelites, 27
Pushkin, A. S., 10, 12, 23, 25, 26, 27, 29, 50, 63, 79, 83, 95, 111, 122, 123, 126, 133 n, 139 n

Ramshev, 5
Realism, 4, 27, 66, 69, 83, 86-87, 105; *see also* "New Realism, The"
Rebus, 64
Reeve, F. (critic), 68-69
Rimbaud, 27, 28, 31, 46
Robinson Crusoe, 11
Romances sans Paroles (Verlaine), 37-38, 39
Romantic Flowers (Romanticheskie tsvety) (Gumilev), 118
Romanticism, 27, 76, 80, 82, 88, 99, 125, 126
Römische Elegien (Goethe), 81
Rossetti, Danti, 87
Rousseau, 46
Rozanov, V., 105
Russian Archive (Russkii arkhiv), 50, 53-54, 64
Russian Froebel Society, 11
Russian Leaflet, The (Russkii listok), 64
Russian Modernism. *See* Modernism
Russian Record, The (Russkie vedomosti), 63
Russian Review, The (Russkoe obozrenie), 29, 34
Russian Social-Revolutionary Library, The, 9
Russian Sport, 19
Russian Symbolism. *See* Symbolism
Russian Symbolists, The (Russkie simvolisty), 3, 30, 31-35, 36, 37, 38, 39, 41, 104, 123;
        reason for publication, 31, reviews of, 31-36; significance of, 38-39
Russian Thought (Russkaia mysl'), 109
Russian Wealth (Russkoe bogatstvo), 6, 33, 35
Russkaia mysl'. See Russian Thought
Russkaia sotsial'no-revoliutsionnaia biblioteka. See Russian Social-Revolutionary Library,
        The
Russkie simvolisty. See Russian Symbolists, The
Russkie vedomosti. See Russian Record, The
Russkii arkhiv. See Russian Archive
Russkii listok. See Russian Leaflet, The
Russkoe bogatstvo. See Russian Wealth
Russkoe obozrenie. See Russian Review, The

Saints' Calendar, 9
Saltykov-Shchedrin, 4, 5
Samygin, 44, 48

Satin, 29

Scales, The (Vesy), 56, 59, 62, 64, 65-66, 78, 91, 114, 135 n. 29 and 34; Briusov's break with, 92, 102, 104, 108-111, 139 n; Briusov's relations with staff of, 103; closing of, 108-114, 118; as creator of the Symbolist movement in Russia, 112; struggle with other Modernist factions, 93, 100, 105-108

Schnitzler, 56

Schopenhauer, 23, 25

"Scientific poetry," 119

"Serious Artist, The" (Pound), 83

Severnye tsvety. See Northern Flowers

Severnyi vestnik. See Northern Herald, The

Shakespeare, 24

Shelgunov, 5

Shestov, Lev, 105

"Shipovnik." See "Sweetbrier"

Silver Age, 5

Silver Dove, The (Blok), 117

"Simvolism i sovremennoe russkoe iskusstvo." See "Symbolism and Contemporary Russian Art"

Sincere Word (Zadushevnoe slovo), 13, 19

"Skorpion" (publishing house), 53, 55-64, 90, 92, 117

Sluchevsky, K., 7, 51

Society of Lovers of Western Literature (Obshchestvo liubitelei zapadnoi literatury), 39

Sokolov, 51

Sologub, 6, 7, 51, 52, 97, 117, 122

Solovyov, S., 109, 110, 117, 122

Solovyov, Vladimir, 7, 31-32, 34, 35, 105, 131 n

Southern Review, The (Yuzhnoe obozrenie), 53

Spinoza, 23, 29, 123

Spirit of Romance, The (Pound), 84

Sports Sheet, The, 19

Staniukovich, Vladimir (childhood friend), 18

Steiner, Rudolf, 110

Stender-Petersen, A. (critic), 6

Stock, Noel (critic), 88

St. Petersburg: differences between St. Petersburg Symbolists and Moscow Symbolists, 37, 61-62, 65, 68, 74, 131 n

Stroev (childhood friend), 16

Sumarokov, 46

Summer Passions (Dachnye strasti), 29-30

Sventsitsky, 105

"Sweetbrier" ("Shipovnik"), 103, 105

Symbolic Realism, 105

Symbolism: ambiguity of meaning, 92; beginnings of Russian Symbolism, 27-29; Briusov's attitudes toward as a school, 70-89 passim, 91, 98-102, 106-108, 112-116; Briusov's contribution to, 122-127; chronological beginning of, 68-70; contrasted to Decadence, 68-69, 102; decline of, 114-119, 141 n; definition of, 67-69; difference between and Modernism, 104-105; difference between and Realism, 86-87; French, 26-29, 65, 68, 101, 136 n, 140 n; "non-theory of," 106-108; philosophy of, according to Bely, 105-107; as polemical synonym for art, 93-94; as Realism, 85, 137 n; relations between Symbolists and Decadents, 57, 61-62; in Russia created by The Scales, 112; transition from to Acmeism, 115, 118; transition from Decadence to, 67; two Russian schools of, 37, 65; uniting Symbolists into a school, 37; see also

[153]

Briusov, Valery Yakovlevich, esthetic views.
"Symbolism and Contemporary Russian Art" ("Simvolizm i sovremennoe russkoe iskusstvo")
(Bely), 104-
"Symbolist Poets in France: Verlaine, Mallarmé, Rimbaud, Laforgue, Moréas, The" (Z.
Vengerova), 27, 28
Symbols (Merezhkovsky), 27, 28, 29

Tailhade, Laurent, 31
Tennyson, 27
Tiutchev, 50, 52, 111, 122; as Symbolists' predecessor, 95-96
Tolstoy, A. K., 26
Tolstoy, L. N., 26, 51, 136 n
"To Our Readers" ("K chitateliam") (*The Scales'* closing statement), 112, 113
Torches (Fakely), 93, 103, 114
Tovarishch. See Comrade
"Tradition and the Individual Talent" (Eliot), 81-82, 125
Tsvetaeva, Marina, 26, 80, 129 n
Turgenev, I. S., 26, 117
Tynianov, Yury (critic), 35

Under Northern Skies (Pod severnym nebom) (Balmont), 39
Universal Illustrated (Vsemirnaia illiustratsiia), 33
Uspensky, Gleb, 5

"Valery Briusov's Juvenilia" ("Iunosheskoe tvorchestvo Valeriia Briusova") (Gudzii), 25
Valéry, Paul, 82, 83-84, 87-88
Vengerova, Z., 27, 28
Verhaeren, 135 n
Verlaine, 27, 28, 29, 37, 70
Verne, Jules, 12, 17
Vestnik Evropy. See Messenger of Europe, The
Vesy. See Scales, The
Vilenkin, N. M. *See* Minsky, N. M.
Vipper, Egor Frantsevich (geography teacher), 15
Virgil, 120
Volynsky, 6
Volzhsky, 105
Vsemirnaia illiustratsiia. See Universal Illustrated

Warren, A. (critic), 87
Weber, 46
Week, The (Nedelia), 33
Wellek. R., 87
West, James (critic), 68-69
White Lily, The (V. Solovyov), 131 n
Wilson, Edmond, 82

Yakovlev, 29
Yakubovich, P. F. *(reviewer for Russian Wealth)*, 35
Yasinsky, Ieronim, 4, 5, 51, 58, 134 n
Yasiuninsky, 29
Yuzhnoe obozrenie. See Southern Review, The

Zadushevnoe slovo. See Sincere Word
Zaria. See Dawn, The
Zhukovsky, 10, 139 n
Zhurnal dlia vsekh. See Journal for All, The
Znamia. See Banner, The
Zoia (governess), 19
Zolotoe runo. See Golden Fleece, The